WOMEN THRIVE

VOLUME III

Inspiring True Stories of Women Overcoming Adversity

RAIMONDA JANKUNAITE

KIM BLYTH

DIANE GILMAN

TAJNI DILLER

LINDA CLARK

ANNA BERARDI

STEPHANIE MYERS

GABS HAYES

EMILY SANDERS

SHAMERIA ANN DAVIS

ANA M. SANTOS

STACIE A. FORD

This book compilation is initiated by Raimonda Jankunaite, the founder of Women Thrive Media Ltd. If you would like to be published as an author in our future book compilations such as this please visit www.womenthrivesummit.com/book or email us at contact@womenthrivemedia.com

Copyright © 2024 by Women Thrive Media Ltd.

Ebook ISBN: 978-1-7384107-3-6
Paperback ISBN: 978-1-7384107-2-9

Cover Art: Rajni Chunara @Lineart_ly
Formatting, Interior Design and Cover Design: Woven Red Author Services

With thanks to the authors and the whole Women Thrive Media team, mentors and editors for their support in bringing this book to life.

The information and advice contained in this book are based upon the research and the personal and professional experiences of the authors. Some names and characteristics have been changed, some events have been compressed, and some dialogue has been recreated.

Chapters reflect the authors' present recollections of experiences over time. The opinions herein are of each individual contributor. All writings are the property of individual contributors. The publisher and authors are not responsible for any adverse effects or consequences resulting from the use of any of the suggestions, preparations, or procedures discussed in this book.

DEDICATION

This book is dedicated to you, the woman who has gone through life's challenges that did not break her. She is strong and determined but may feel a little broken inside. Maybe there are shadow parts she has not yet discovered about herself.

This is for a woman who aspires for more in life, despite the pains and struggles she has faced, that was meant to break here.
But she is here, to be a testimony of what is possible.

You may be here because you discovered this by chance, or a friend has given you a copy of this book, or perhaps you know one of the authors. Just know that within the pages of this book is exactly what you need to read right now.

To a woman who wants to thrive in life and wants to be inspired by other women rising to their power and purpose in life.

For a woman who wants to become aligned, live a purposeful life and create the freedom to be who she was created to be. Be unapologetically you.

"A butterfly cannot see its wings, but the rest of us can. Remember: you are beautiful, and while you may not see it, we can."

Do you feel inspired to share highlights of this book on social media? We would love for you to use hashtag #WomenThriveBook and tag us @womenthrivemedia

To get to know our authors and to express interest to share your story, please visit www.womenthrivesummit.com/book

TABLE OF CONTENTS

WHY THIS BOOK EXISTS

At Women Thrive Media, we publish stories of inspiring women who have overcome adversities in life. Our mission is to create a platform and a stage where every woman can have the opportunity to share her story. Via our book series we get the opportunity to spotlight women's stories, from all across the world.

Over the years of working with hundreds of women, we have seen more similarities than differences in our experiences, stories, struggles and traumas.

It is by having the courage to share our stories with others that we liberate ourselves of silence and empower ourselves and others to stand rooted in our truth. This book is a personal recollection of women's life events, personal struggles, inner dialog and incredible transformation.

The process of writing this book for the authors was healing and liberating, transformational, and today, you as a reader get to be the witness of their stories in print.

This book exists so you as a reader may be inspired, connected and motivated by the women's stories and feel less alone in your life struggles. We hope this book finds space on your bookshelf, bedside chest of drawers, coffee table, or library alongside other inspirational books.

Please gift this book to another woman and help us continue sharing inspiring true stories of women overcoming adversities with the world, so we can show how strong and resilient women are.

Through our WOMEN THRIVE book series, we hope to give as many women the opportunity to write their stories and inspire the world with words of encouragement. Sharing stories of overcoming adversities in life and finding the way forward to rise and thrive.

If you would like to contribute to our future Women Thrive Book series, please visit www.womenthrivesummit.com/book, where you will find our interest form.

INTRODUCTION

Dear Reader,

This anthology has been created by twelve, amazing women from different parts of the world, backgrounds and life experiences. While they didn't know each other before investing their passion and truth into this project, they all shared something in common. And that something was a mission to positively impact others through the power of their stories.

Some of these stories have not been shared before. We thank our authors for being brave enough to pour their hearts out to you, dear reader, in the hope that by doing so they'll make a positive difference in your life. It takes a lot of courage, soul searching, self-questioning and doubting to speak our truth. To lay our challenges and our trials bare for someone else to read and experience is an act of bravery that cannot be underestimated. It requires reliving our stories and committing ourselves to inner healing.

You may not resonate with all of these stories right now, but the story that touches you least today may be exactly the one you need to hear in years to come. It may hold the wisdom that you require for a future challenging experience. The purpose of this book is to inspire you and to remind you that life comes with adversities, unexpected twists and turns, and sometimes the path is very rocky indeed. There will be times when you're riding high on life and seem to have it all. Then, life just pulls the rug out from under your feet.

This book aims to give you the strength and inspiration to KEEP GO-ING despite the challenges. And to triumph over adversity. For some, the start in life was not as fortunate as it could be. And some of these women could have been stuck on a trajectory of tragedy. For others, adversity came later in life, bringing valuable lessons and teaching that purpose can be found in pain.

These authors have experienced some truly trying times that nearly broke them. But in those moments of defeat and despair, they found strength, awakening and a will of steel to survive and come through the other side. Stronger than ever. As you read the pages of this book, re-member that this could be someone's survival guide. Share this guide. Gift it to your friends and loved ones. Leave a review, tell us how this book has touched your life. Send a message to an author (or authors) that have really moved you with their story.

I promise you that is the most rewarding part of writing a book. Hav-ing our readers tell us just how much our words have meant to them. It is the biggest gift and blessing to have our stories out in the world, touching people's lives.

Now, take a few moments to really look at the pictures on the cover. There may be one face that 'speaks' to you today. And the next time you hold this book in your hand, another face may resonate with you. This anthology is designed to take you on an inspirational journey, an experience where every time you read it you'll discover something new about the author, their story, or yourself.

As you tread your own path, take your own journey, may this book be a companion. And a reminder of just how strong, resilient, and capa-ble we all are of overcoming adversities and finding our way through them, to shine and thrive.

Raimonda Jankunaite

1

THE POWER OF YOUR VOICE

RAIMONDA JANKUNAITE

A s I write this beautiful chapter and invite you to discover our collective stories in this book. May this book bring you new revelations about other women from all around the world and about parts of yourself that you may not know exist yet. I hope you discover something that inspires you and connects to deeper parts of you that opens opportunity for reflection and healing.

I mentor hundreds of women every year to help them heal through the power of sharing their stories with the world. I create a safe space for women to share their stories with the world and I do so through book mentoring and coaching, publishing, speaker training and our global events. I have been in business since 2011 and have travelled around the sun 35 times as well as done many air miles visiting the most beautiful parts of the world.

I have been fortunate to meet many incredible women in my life and witness them on stages and in their moment of healing, growth and accepting their truth. I often attract women who share the same values and are also on a mission or quest to change the world in their own unique ways. I believe that my traumas and life experiences have helped me soften my heart and have more empathy and compassion for others. I have learnt that we have all been through life's challenges and dealing with so many struggles on a daily basis.

Whilst there are so many global challenges that are facing us right now, and an incredible divide globally, I want women to become a united voice of hope, healing, compassion and unity. I always say, there is so much more that unites us than separates us, and together we can be the change in the world.

My true passion is to empower women to have a voice and build a platform and a stage for women to have a place to share their messages with the world. I love to amplify women's stories, achievements and expertise so we can inspire the next generation of great leaders and entrepreneurs. Via the Women Thrive Books we have created a magical community of women who are all ambitious and share the same vision of women's empowerment. Together, we plan to host more in-person events for women in order to foster a community and support network of women for women.

In the coming years, we plan to host global Thrive Talks events featuring incredible women in our community so you can be inspired by their stories and purposeful missions. Every year, we have over a thousand applicants wanting to speak and feature on our stage. These women include successful business owners, coaches, entrepreneurs, authors, creatives. All who have unique stories and missions.

I believe that we have all been given a mission in life and it usually transpires through our own life experiences often times finding meaning and purpose in our most challenging moments. Sometimes we have to experience the loss of our own identity in order to find new purpose and meaning in our lives. It is in the messy parts of our story that we can find greatness within ourselves that allows us to have a breakthrough and survive the unimaginable.

In writing the Women Thrive Book series, I have shared many moments of my own personal life and challenges. In Volume I, I shared my story of 'Starting a New Chapter', finding my purpose, and meaning and embarking on a new life in Spain after a relationship breakup. In Volume II, I shared my childhood story of being a young immigrant girl with a dream that I made a reality and how the women in my life contributed to my vision now.

In this chapter I share the story of how I've struggled with depression and faced traumas in my mid-20s that left me with low confidence, loss of identity and my voice. I never knew that something profound can happen in your life and it could rip you of your most precious thing, your voice and identity. I also never knew how many others have also been affected by similar circumstances or struggled with the same thing until I started to share my story with the world.

I asked myself many times: *Why am I here? Who was I created to be? What can I do with my life to leave my footprints on this earth?*

These were the profound questions I asked myself over and over again when I was searching for my life's purpose again after my trauma. It was these questions that helped me step my foot forward again and pursue something more than 'Me'.

So in 2020 I established Women Thrive as a collective women's platform, a community, events and publications like our magazine and books for women. My mission is to inspire women to share their authentic stories and life wisdom with the world, so others can feel less alone in their life's challenges and struggles.

I know you will probably see parts of your own life and struggles in someone else's story as you read the chapters in this book. You will probably connect with some of the authors in this book in more profound ways than others. Their stories may trigger a feeling or emotion within you. Be open to exploring and growing through the pages of this book.

I hope that you one day also feel encouraged to share your own story and inspire others with your words. It is a profound experience, one that many of our authors found healing, transformation and growth.

Ask yourself...How would your life change if you shared your story? How could your life change if you could unapologetically step into your true and authentic self? How could you change the lives of others if you spoke your truth?

My life changed when I became empowered and unapologetic to share my story. I have built a business that not only lives in alignment with my life purpose and mission but also leaves a lasting legacy for many others. Finding my voice in the world and being able to use it to inspire and motivate others, has been my most profound transformation.

When You Look in the Mirror, What Do You See?

There was a moment in my life when I looked in the mirror and didn't recognise myself. The woman looking back at me was just a shell of the woman I had known. The young, dynamic, confident, happy and out-going me was hiding behind pain, shame and guilt. As I looked at myself in the mirror I cried, "Rai, please speak." But I could not find the words to express how I felt inside.

I could not get the sound of my voice out. I felt silenced. I hid in my home, struggling to even get out of bed on some days. I did not know at the time, but I was suffering from depression. I felt broken on the inside. I blamed myself for my decisions that led me here and I felt ashamed. What if people really found out the truth?

I could not tell anyone what I was going through. The sense of what what going on within me was unbearable yet, not something I could not find the words or courage to speak about to anyone. My overwhelming emotions and shame had locked my voice and confidence away and I felt broken. I did not know where to seek help. I believed that being mistreated and violated in a relationship was perhaps my own doing and I had to bear the outcome of it.

I know that society often blames women for being entangled with more powerful and successful men and therefore being subjected to mistreatment is almost expected therefore disempowering us on having a voice and never speaking our truth. I was sadly in one of those society judged relationships where I found myself unexpectedly trapped.

He was rich, controlling, jealous, manipulative and overbearing. Surely, these dating websites should put a warning when joining that you will find some rich but broken men on this platform. No doubt he had some healing to do but he knew what he wanted and there was nothing to stop him, and I was on his radar. The young, beautiful, edu-cated, ambitious and somewhat naive 'Eastern European' woman that fitted his ideal for a wife material. He has had a long career and become very successful, with a home base in Manhattan and Long Island, and additional homes in the South of France and Tunisia, that was his coun-try of origin. When I met him, I was at a verge of shutting down my first business, I was broken, and I felt like a failure. A man with a golden ticket, you may think?

Well for me at the time was survival and temporary escape from my dire situation. So over the months of speaking online with him, I got roped into his vision of having a fantastic life together and a loving relationship.

Of course, on the outset it looked like a movie, lifestyle any *'girl'* would dream of. But I was becoming a woman of my own, and freedom, authenticity and truth were some of the few of my values. Everything about going with an older man for his wealth just felt wrong to me, even if it was right by him. I could not imagine introducing my 40 years older husband to my family or friends. I can't even recall how many years separated us, but it felt a lot and it was visibly so. On one end I was being seduced by him and the glamorous lifestyle, living in New York City in brand new apartments, travelling the world first class, having unlimited credit card and on the other end of the spectrum, feeling deeply trapped under a man's thumb. No matter how much I could see his caring and nurturing side, I couldn't love him the way I knew I could. I am a leo woman, so I knew I could love deeply and passionately.

Whilst we had some amazing trips together, most of them ended in arguments and me walking out to find my own way home. Every time I felt overly controlled or pushed, I would walk out and assert my independence. Even if it meant putting myself into dangerous situations. This frustrated him. I was 'out of his control' and at times it infuriated him. I would use the famous words - 'You can't buy my love' and create rather dramatic scenes of woman's worth. I never wanted to be controlled, I always knew that we women secretly hold the power and, if we are smart enough, we would use it to navigate our lives and relationships successfully.

Of course, I could speak now in retrospect but at times I wasn't always able to hold the power torch and often felt overpowered and defeated. It was a power struggle between two people trying to pull in different directions and I was losing the battle.

The Final Walk Out

I was dropped off at an airport in Tunisia by my then boyfriend's driver and left to find my own way home. No ticket. No belongings. No money.

It was the conclusion of my three-year rocky relationship with a powerful, rich and narcissistic man whose dream was to make me a trophy wife. A man who had flown me around the world to show off his acquired homes, political and business influence and money. A man I had met on SugarDaddy.com. I was not proud of it, but it is the truth.

At the airport I called my sister and asked her to help me get home. It was the ultimate shame to ask my family to bail me out of a situation I had put myself into. When I got home to London, I could not speak. I locked myself away in my apartment and cried.

How could I be so naive and think that there was a possibility of having a healthy relationship with a man who only wanted me as his trophy wife? He had the intention to have me as an accessory in his life. Man who believed that money can buy him everything including a wife.

I did not know that the one encounter on a dating app would turn my world upside down, and not in ways that I had ever expected. Three years later finding out for myself how 'Mr Wrong' can leave you with scars and a new meaning in your life. This will forever be my biggest mistake and the biggest blessing that transpired from it that enabled me to step into my purpose.

I ended up in Tunisia, with the intention of that being my final visit to collect my things that I'd left behind when I fled our stay in Cannes in his home. It was yet another argument that caused me to walk out and get a flight home. I knew that this visit would be my last, and he knew that too. The relationship was beyond repair, and I wanted out.

On the last day of the trip, he hosted a dinner party with some of his powerful friends to show me off as his future trophy wife telling everyone that one day I will be baring his children. At the end of the evening, I felt embarrassed and told him not to speak about our relationship to his friends like that, when we both knew we were not planning any of it.

He was infuriated and of course knew that he would never see me again, so the morning after I missed my flight home, he made sure to 'make love to me' one last time and do so like a dirty animal. It was his way to 'destroy' our relationship and leave me feeling ripped off of my dignity. It felt disgusting and overwhelming. Afterwards, I went to the shower and cried, he left and sent me a driver to take me to the airport.

This last incident is what triggered my trauma and deep attachment to feeling worthless, broken and disgusted with myself, for allowing someone to get close and physical with me that I no longer had desire to be with. Knowing that he simply wanted to have the last physical interaction with me to rip me off my soul.

I was in such a dark place after the incident, yet I could not quite put my finger on why I was feeling the way I was feeling. All I knew was that now I was different. Something had profoundly changed within me. I could not say it was a rape or an incident that happened by accident and so I found no place for my voice.

I Was No Longer the Woman I Was Before

I felt empty and soulless.

I felt like my entire identity had been torn away and I could not see my purpose in the world. I struggled to put my words together. I struggled to trust myself. I could not even talk to myself, let alone others.

I had no idea how I would find my way back, so I stood still. Silent. Broken. Alone. I did not know what healing looked like. So I did what I knew best, I tried to move on and rebuild my life. I asked myself questions of my purpose in the world and how I could make a difference.

It was a slow and lonely journey. I had to pretend I was ok for a long while and try to carry on with life, hiding behind the pain I was feeling. I would go out socialising and smile, but deep inside I struggled every second of the day. It was like a movie in my head replaying the same story over and over again.

Pain, guilt, fear and shame. Fear of being found out that 'the perfect woman' on the outside was so broken on the inside. That despite her big ambitions in life she did not know who she was inside. Despite wanting to be motivational for others, I could not muster the words to inspire myself. I questioned everything, including my own existence.

It was in my deepest struggle that I found my inner warrior. I searched for new meaning, new purpose and direction. It did not come quickly; it came through slow progress of daily actions to reaffirm to myself that I had something within me that would keep me going. That my pain and struggle did not define me. That my failure was not final and the further I went, the more headway I could make. Confidence was hard to build back up again after the incident and lack of belief from my closest did not help.

One day, my sister looking at me with pity said, *"If I was you, I would get a job at the local supermarket. At least you would be doing something with your life."*. That was the lowest blow for me at the time.

I knew I was smart, and I knew I had ideas that could become something. I wasn't afraid of hard work either. Having been an immigrant in the UK, there was no way I was going back to the lowest-paid jobs to survive. Despite being broken, I still had my self-worth, and I could not see myself standing at the checkout and serving people with a smile. I could not accept that as my reality.

I was not only internally broken, but I was also broke. I had no job, no viable business to hold on to at the time. I searched for a new direction, but nothing was forthcoming. I had to take control of my life. I had to put my failures behind me, in order to go forward. I was unemployable because I had chosen an entrepreneurial journey early in my career and I was stuck. I had a choice - build my own business *or* take low-paid jobs and accept defeat.

Those words from my sister hurt me deeply but also fuelled me. As they say, when someone does not believe in you, prove them wrong. So I gathered all that I had left of me to find a way through. I cut down on all my expenses, defaulted on all my financial commitments and started to rebuild my life from scratch. I remember seeing a homeless man on the street begging for money and thinking, you are richer than me, at least you don't have debt hanging over you. I felt sorry for myself, but I knew that self-pity could lead you nowhere. I needed a plan.

Finding New Purpose

So I continued to search within myself for my next breakthrough idea. I got myself a consulting position with my mentor's company, a small boutique turnaround company that was working with various businesses. The businesses we were working with were raising millions in funding, and so I committed myself to learn everything there was to learn about money, success and how to build a business. I sat in meetings with investors, clients, and teams. I helped close deals securing funding for companies. I was good at my job and found meaning again in my work.

In my 20's in business, I've met many people and some less amazing ones who would be more inclined to waste your time as a woman with a business agenda. I would be invited for coffee to talk about business and get nowhere in real business conversation because men would be assuming of other intentions or ideas. I've 'kissed many frogs' in the business world, as they say. I was growing frustrated trying to thrive in this environment. Even though some of the funding round deals we were closing paid very well, they were taking much time and effort to bring to conclusion. I dreamed of a business of my own doing something that I truly love.

Fore me, freedom is one of my core values - it is the underpinning theme in my life, both professionally and personally. I strive for freedom in my life, that is why I have decided to start my own business at the age of 21 and dedicate so many years to building my own business. I could not see myself ever working for anyone else, or as a woman have to be ruled by 9-5 working commitment.

When I think about the word Freedom I can not only pinpoint specific stories from my life that shaped this belief in me, such as coming from a family of self starter business owners and entrepreneurs, being an immigrant in the UK at the early age of 13 and having to fight for my own freedom. I can give you many different examples of my life choices that led to freedom and therefore self-empowerment, which is particularly important for women in today's world.

So it is no surprise that I do the work that I do today, because it is underpinned by my life experiences, stories and beliefs that have led me to where I am today. So when I speak on stage I can draw from those stories, backed by my key values and purpose in life that I found through the experience of losing my voice. Now I am able to transform and inspire others to speak their authentic truth.

The Unexpected Beginnings

I was working as a consultant in my mid 20's on a 'company rescue' project to rescue a business, restructure their management team and help rebuild their crowdfunding platform. The business was in a bit of a mess because their platform capabilities did not meet their initial vision and they were coming up to the end of their licence to trade as a funding platform. I met the founders at a business tradeshow, and they hired me to support their platform launch, soon realising that it needed a whole rebuild I advised them that it was simply not feasible to launch.

So, I started helping them build a new team, re-write their business plan for the next phase of the business and potential funding round. But quickly after, their existing management team fell apart, and I was suddenly left with the project to do as I pleased so I took ownership of. The owners simply let go and I was left with a team that I've built and plan that I wrote ready to execute. I have always been an entrepreneur at heart, and this was simply an amazing opportunity to something that I love. This was one of those moments that you just have to take a leap of faith and give it a shot. Maybe, just maybe it will all work out.

I went on to re-brand and I created a brand called Crowd Velocity with a mission to give entrepreneurial dreams velocity and funding to launch off the ground. I dreamed of what it would be like to support other entrepreneurs with their entrepreneurial dreams, helping them source funds to support their missions. I envisioned to build a peer-to-peer platform where people could fund each other projects and pool money together for various initiatives. It sparked a fire in me because I knew just how hard it is being a self-starter entrepreneur with limited funds to bring your ideas to life.

It was a business idea that aligned with my values, and I could see how my passion and experience could intersect. I always wanted to be in business, and this would give me an opportunity to work with many amazing entrepreneurs and ideas. After all, I spent my early 20s building my own business, mentoring others and pursuing my dreams. I knew that entrepreneurs are dream sellers and we have to find a way to show others out dreams before they even exist in the world.

This time I was determined to make it work. So, I invested all my time and the little resources that I had from my consulting work to make this crowdfunding project work. I had a co-founder and a small team who were all working for equity (a share in the business), and I found several projects that were willing to fund using our platform. They knew we were a start-up platform, but they were willing to give it a go and I was willing to mentor their project launches to success.

I gathered 5 projects on our newly built platform and decided it was soon time to launch. I had a small (few hundred) email list and a good network of people from all the networking I've done at events and online. I decided to host a launch event for our projects and our new platform. Instead of calling it what it was - 'crowdfunding launch event' - I called it Women in Business. After all, the projects I was supporting were mainly led by women. My goal was to showcase them at this event and launch their funding projects into the world, in the hope that we could raise some significant amounts to launch our platform.

The event was a huge success, we didn't have enough seats for the number of people who booked in to attend! The energy in the room was buzzing, and the presentations and talks went extremely well. At the end of the event, we celebrated and many of the women asked me - when is the next event? I hadn't thought about it. I did not know where we would go from there. But the success of this event gave me an indication of what people wanted.

They did not want to crowdfund, they did not want to invest in projects, and they did not care to be investors nor raise money for their own ideas. They wanted community, connection and the ability to share their experiences. They wanted to feel less alone and be inspired by other people in the room. They loved the ability to connect, network and explore ideas. It was my lightbulb moment. I realised that this was the start of something - I wasn't sure what yet - that had potential.

After the crowdfunding platform launch, I re-evaluated our plans and realised that we had no business. It would require us to raise millions for others in order to sustain ourselves, and for a clunky start-up platform with hardly any projects and no audience, it was simply too steep a hill to climb. I pulled the trigger and told my team and business partner that our plan and platform weren't feasible and that we should transform it into an online learning platform where we could teach entrepreneurs about marketing, visibility and fundraising.

At this time, I was seeing real growth in the Women in Business community and Facebook group and my personal relations with my community strengthened. Women wanted to connect with me and I was having conversations every day with others doing amazing things. No one I was connecting was showing any interest in fundraising, but they were all interested in community, events and building relations to collaborate. It was also clear that the online learning community was growing and opening new opportunities especially for women led platforms.

I hosted another event and this time I focused more on marketing, visibility, personal branding and thought leadership. This was the first event I 'became' a speaker, when I for the first time shared my 'origin story', moment of failure and defeat in my previous business and owned my truth. It was defining moment and definitely daunting to finally wear your mistakes or failures as a badge of honour, wisdom and experience. I did not know it at the time that speaking and sharing my knowledge would become such an intricate part of my journey and mission.

A year later, I hosted my first virtual summit, featuring 14 incredible speakers. The event attracted a few hundred attendees. I raised money for the Best Beginnings charity, championed by Catherine, Duchess of Cornwall and Cambridge. It is through this event that I was inspired to start a women's membership platform and support other women in business. It was pretty clear where my efforts were going so I told my mentor and business partner at the consulting firm that I was leaving and starting out on my own. My last funding project payout was the starting budget I needed to build my new website, invest something in my branding, hire my first VA and set out on my own to build a membership platform. I set up our social media accounts, did my research and made a commitment to show up every day on Instagram. I started making daily inspirational posts and our audience grew.

I spent hours upon hours following and engaging with other accounts, nurturing our audience, creating content and planning our next events, and the launch of the Women in Business Club. It was thrilling - our launch was a success, yet the sign-ups for the platform continued to be slow. Nevertheless, I was determined and could see that what I'd started from a seed of an idea now had real potential. All the signs were there that I was on to something. In the first 3 months, I grew my following to 10k and people started to take notice. The growth continued and every month I gained another 10k followers, then another 20k, and at the year mark, I had grown my account to 100k followers.

This huge milestone helped me open doors to opportunities, collaborations and clients. I started to sell my programs about visibility and Instagram growth. I was becoming established in the online space and started to grow my team and run my own webinars and workshops. I learnt as much as I could about building websites, sales pages, funnels, email campaigns, and so much more. Everything I was learning; I was also teaching others. I was interviewing experts so I could learn from their success and also build the content for our Women in Business members and community. After 3 years of running workshops, I had so much content that I did not know what to do with it. I helped 100s of women build their own businesses through mentoring and our workshops, trained lots of our team members and see some huge success stories come out after our events.

The Beginning of Women Thrive

It was autumn 2019 when we had our second major Women in Business event in London. I had women flying in from all around the world to be there as speakers and attendees. By now, I had a strong brand and supportive community. Women wanted to meet me in person and be part of the experience we were creating. Every week I would get messages from women from all around the world asking if we could host an event in the USA, Australia, Europe, South Africa and many other places. It was evident that women wanted community and they wanted our events locally. So, I set out to expand globally, fixing dates for international events and planning our first event in Atlanta, GA. It was meant to take place in March 2020, and I had spent the previous 3 months relentlessly planning, networking, organising and promoting the event. But something was looming.

There was a world event unfolding beyond anyone's control. It quickly spiralled from being a virus in China to a global pandemic on our doorsteps. Lockdowns started to be introduced in various cities, and people were becoming more and more hesitant to travel and afraid to leave homes. I saw our event ticket sales stalling and the more news I watched about the virus, I realised that we were going nowhere. With a heavy heart, I made the announcement to our team and our community that the event would be cancelled.

My announcement was met with an outpour of support and private messages from women saying they had been quietly praying that I would not have to cancel the event. I had invested so much time and energy into and my commitment to it was 100 percent. The outpour of support helped me pick myself back up and realise that I had bigger work on my hands and my work was done yet.

During the pandemic women were particularly hard hit by the lockdown as now we had become full-time carers for our households and children. Many were considering what they would have to do with their careers and business. Even more people were starting to realise and pivot to new directions and experiencing personal awakenings. I knew that everyone in my community shared the same concerns, experiences and setbacks. I decided to pivot our in-person event in Atlanta into a virtual summit. Something I had wanted to do for a while, but I was so focused on in-person events that I simply had no good reason to start hosting them online, until now.

This was the moment that turned all of our businesses online, and so Women Thrive was born. In the face of adversity, my goal was to help women rise and thrive despite the uncertainty and challenges ahead. I gathered 34 women to speak on my virtual summit stage and it was the most profound event, reaching thousands of women globally. It allowed me to give 34 women from all around the world the opportunity to speak on our stage and attract clients, and support nearly 2000 people in their businesses. I made the commitment to make the Women Thrive Summit our annual female empowerment event; an opportunity for women to come together to share ideas, support each other, be inspired and grow.

My struggles were long behind me. I had learnt to overcome my fear of speaking and managed to rebuild myself. I built a business that I felt so aligned with and passionate about. It felt easy and in-flow. I was the happiest I had been in a long time and, finally, I was living my dream. Personally, I was in yet another challenging relationship, that would spin me in highs and lows. It was controlling, manipulative and dishonest. It was a relationship that saved me from my depression but put me in yet another dysfunctional relationship that was another big lesson and pivotal experience in my journey.

Dare to Dream

Before my second annual Women Thrive summit in 2021, I met my mentor, Les Brown. I had enrolled in this 'Hungry to Speak' programme that was all about public speaking. I was thrilled to find myself in such a high calibre mentoring container with a legend. I would show up to every call despite it being in the middle of the night for me. When I had the opportunity to personally speak to Les Brown, I told him about my

Women Thrive event and the work I do to support women in business. I told him how passionate I was about speaking, events and empowering other women to have a voice.

It was then Les turned to me and asked, "Ok, so you are doing all of this amazing work, that is very inspirational. But why do you want to speak?" A natural question for someone enrolling in a speaking program. It was then that I came face to face with my trauma. In a split second, I said, "Mr Les, I want to speak because I know what it's like not to have a voice." He asked me to expand.

Up until this point, I never told anyone about my experience of depression and losing my voice due to trauma. It was a story I had long buried within me and vowed to never ever tell anyone. No one knew about my ex who in some way caused me distress and how deeply that incident impacted my mental health. No one knew that I had lost my identity, that I profoundly struggled to speak, and how hard I had worked to build myself back up again. No one knew the courage I had to muster to start using my voice and find the strength to speak at my own events.

In that moment, it finally made sense why I do what I do and why I am so passionate about seeing other women have a voice. It is why I am so driven to support women in becoming speakers and authors and women who are empowered to speak their truth. Finally, for the first time, I spoke my truth. Finally, I could take off my mask, accept my story, and realise that my story was not for me, it was for others to draw inspiration from.

My peers on that call went absolutely crazy in the chat to show their support and to share their emotions of being deeply touched by my story. From that moment on, I had my 'fans' in the Hungry to Speak community who had my back and encouraged me to keep on sharing my story and pursuing my goals and mission. Speaking and sharing my story wasn't easy but I was on my way. The belief and encouragement from my peers strengthened my conviction, hunger and determination. I believe that Les Brown is one of the great leaders who taught me compassionate leadership, kindness and the power of vision. The program challenged me to go deeper, to face my shadows and begin more meaningful transformational work on myself and for others.

Whilst my career was taking off, there was one thing that was still holding me back. I wasn't living my truth. I was disempowered under my own roof. I was championing women and their voices but at home I was still silenced. My partner was controlling, mentally and financially. He was not honest and made sure I was kept away from his 'other' life. Often times my devices were tapped for my location, sound and messages so I regularly felt under control and surveillance, and it felt intense. I knew my time in this relationship was coming to an end when I saw my true purposeful life passing me by in another parallel life, and the longer I avoided making the leap the further away from my aligned life I was travelling.

I had to time my 'escape' or departure. Before I could do that, knowing I would be displaced, I had two more projects to deliver, our annual Women Thrive Summit in March for our community, and the Dare to Dream event for Les Brown where we were spotlighting our speakers. As crazy as it sounds, I knew making a leap before I was ready would turn my entire world upside down and I was not wrong.

As a leader and host of these events I had to show up empowered, lead the way, and inspire people with my message so I had to hold it together for a little while longer. All the while I knew deep down, I was living a lie. I knew that if I wanted to become truly empowered in my voice and live my truth, I had to escape my life and the relationship I was in.

And so the day of the Dare to Dream speakers event came and it was the most incredible, profound and impactful event I have ever hosted. A dream come true; hosting an event alongside some of the most amazing inspirational speakers with the legendary Les Brown headlining the event. My professional life was flying high. I couldn't, however, say the same about my personal life.

I was now stepmum to my partner's daughter, and his ex, the daughter's mother, was also living under my roof as I prepared for my 'walk out'. She had drinking problems and I was baby sitting not only our step-daughter but also her mum with somewhat unpredictable, and self-destructive behaviour patterns. I was hosting her in my home all whilst working long hours and preparing for my relationship ending. Despite all of these dynamics and overwhelm of fear and emotions I continued to hold it all together and maintain my commitments.

Until the day after the event, when my partner called me in the morning and told me that he had listened in on our conversation on our home camera that we installed for his daughter and that he was not happy with me lying to him about what time I had gone to bed the night before.

The truth is, I did not go to bed the night before. I was in such a high from the event I could not sleep so I ended up staying up all night talking to his ex about her own childhood experiences, parenting, traumas and how her relationship ended with my ex. I saw some irregularities in the story and of course confirmation of some suspicions. She shared stories with me that were deeply personal and before we knew it it was dawn. So when my boyfriend called, I had told him that I just got up trying to avoid having to explain the conversations we have had.

When he started to question me and tell me I was a liar, for me was the final straw, being controlled and watched in my own home just felt too much to take. I knew this was the beginning of a new chapter for me, a story which I shared in the Volume I of the Women Thrive Book of how I walked free and created a new life for myself.

Finding My Superpower in My Voice

What I know now is that no one is going to empower us unless we empower ourselves, by taking our own power back. For me, the journey began when I started to speak my truth of what happened to me, when I started to shed the shame, guilt and fear. When I accepted myself and all of my past mistakes and let go of everything that was in any way controlling me or manipulating me. I now know what a healthy relationship looks like, and how important it is for us to own our truth. It is the most profound change within yourself when empowerment comes from within you.

I have helped many women write their pain-to-purpose stories. Every time you step more into your authentic self, you are introduced to new versions of yourself that you may never have known existed. It is the butterfly effect of sharing our truth. When you transform, you renew; the 'old' you must die in order for the 'new' you to emerge. It is amazing to witness women stepping into their unapologetic selves, especially when they share their stories with the world because they speak from a place of empowerment and wisdom and no longer from a place of pain. When women stop hiding behind shame, fear or guilt and step into their true authentic sleeves.

Believe, Achieve, Inspire

The words I live by are: Believe, Achieve, Inspire. They are not just words; they are the components of success. I started my first business at the age of 21, I dedicated my entire 20s and now 30s to business and entrepreneurship. I took the high road from ever pursuing a normal 9-5 career and defined my own success. I have had times when it was hard to keep on going, and belief was one thing that got me through many challenging days. Even when there is no hope, or no one is cheering for you, you can always hold on to belief.

Entrepreneurs are dream sellers because we have to believe that our dream or idea is real and then convince others that 'that thing' exists and sell it. If people believe in you and your product, they will buy it. But if you are going to be waiting for your dream to happen for you, you will be waiting a long time. If you're an entrepreneur, you will see your vision and go after it against all odds.

That is the next part of my mantra, Achieve - be so good they can't ignore you. Make your dreams happen, pursue them fearlessly and see them come to life. I recently found my vision board from a few years ago. It was so amazing to see how my own vision evolved and the different paths that I have taken to achieve my dream. That's the thing about achieving success, it may not always happen how you envisioned it but you will get what you have asked for.

The last part is Inspire - and for me that means giving back, sharing our stories and learnings and inspiring other people around us. Making an impact, raising others by raising our standards ourselves. Stepping into leadership and being of service to others.

I speak on many stages and often meet women who have big dreams and goals but are not stepping into their true purpose and power because of fear; fear of judgement, fear of success, fear of transformation. I know that stepping into your power is a big leap of faith. It means being strong in your vulnerabilities, standing in your conviction, and pursuing something meaningful and purposeful. I love it when women come and share their big vision goals with me, and I see them achieve those goals and more.

I have been around the sun for 35 years now, and I can tell you that the most inspiring women are women who are comfortable in their own being. They are authentic, deeply connected to their mission and living life with purpose. When you meet a woman like that you know that this woman has arrived, she is the queen. But often, people don't see the struggles behind many of our smiles and grand achievements. There is always an opportunity cost and this woman no doubt has been through the trenches of business and life experiences.

I invite you to explore what makes you who you are today.

Is it the accolades? Is it the home, cars or clothes you wear? Is it the titles you attach to yourself?

What defines you? Does society define you or do YOU define yourself?

If you could write a narrative for your story - what would it be today and into the future?

We so often live by definitions. What does today's successful, independent businesswoman look like? What does an empowered woman look like? What defines her success?

For me, my definition of success is how many lives I have touched in a positive way. It helps them see that their definition of life and themselves is the most powerful one that they get to tell.

What If You Could Change the World?

If you really tapped into your heart right now and asked yourself, 'What hill am I prepared to die on?'. What is my truth that I could wholeheartedly live by till the end of time with passion and conviction? You become unshakable when you live your truth, and you are willing to die standing by your conviction. Of course, in life not every battle is matter of life or death, but your purpose in life could be.

I know that the women who finally choose to speak up and share their stories make ripple effect in the world. We can change lives, save lives and make sure that other women don't have to go through the same experiences as we have had to. Life happens to all of us, not just some of us. But only a few choose to speak about their life experiences courageously.

No matter if people may judge me or you, no matter if some may not hear or resonate with your story, remember it is meant for someone and it is your responsibility to make sure it is shared.

If you only had 180 days to live, what would you do? Would you care about anyone's opinions, or would you spend your time pursuing your dreams and living life fully as your true authentic self?

When I tapped into this urgency in my own life, it opened a new world of possibilities for me. I started to say YES to things that made a difference and NO to things that did not matter. I started to get intentional about building a legacy business. I grew my business from 5 people to over 20 people. I started to act with urgency and the universe delivered.

So, why not live your life as if you only have 180 days left to live; this will inspire you to pursue things you have perhaps always been afraid to pursue, step into your purpose and become unapologetic about making decisions and moving forward. Right now - live the life you've always wanted to live. Not only your life would change but you would change many lives by simply pursuing your own dreams and being unapologetically yourself.

What If Women Could Change the World?

If you want to see the difference in the world, you must first start with you. Grow things that you love within you, create things you aspire to in life, and see how the external world will start to change. When we change our internal environment, from the inner chatter to a more empowered and confident outlook on life, we give and attract more of the same in the world.

So life around us can change when we step into our own greatness. What if you could plant a seed of hope, transformation and inspiration for others? What if the action you took today could be the seed that sprouts some months later? What action would you commit to taking every day that could change the world?

For me, it is inspiring others and empowering women to be authentically magnetic and unapologetically themselves. What if that one commitment would be speaking and advocating for your mission and purpose in life? How many lives could it change? That is the power of sharing your story.

Raimonda Jankunaite

Raimonda Jankunaite is the founder and CEO at Women thrive Media, she is an international speaker, best-selling author, magazine editor and publisher, also known as a Visibility Queen and Global Changemarker. She is the visionary founder of the Women Thrive Summit, an annual women empowerment event featuring 50+ speakers, entrepreneurs, visionary leaders and early-stage speakers. She spent the last 15 years pursuing entrepreneurial dreams and building a platform for women.

Today, she is a thought leader, visionary leader and champion of women voices. She is Manifestor in human design and is able to bring people together towards one unified mission and movement. Her passion is travel and hosting retreat and creating unforgettable experiences for women. Since 2020 Raimonda has worked with more than 350 speakers, 20 authors and hosted over 500 hours of events and workshops.

Her mission is to impact 1 million women lives every year, through the Women Thrive Books, Magazine, Podcast, events and the community and mentorship. She runs various visibility programs and support speakers and authors with visibility, media and public speaking skills, so more women can become self advocates, thought leaders and great story tellers.

2

MY AWAKENING: THE UNVEILING OF BURIED MEMORIES

KIM BLYTHE

"The power of the story lies not just in the words but the strength it gives to those who listen." ~ Unknown

I did something last year out of character for me, to celebrate my awakening. My husband, Mark, and I took a life-changing trip to Greece with some friends, traveling to Athens and cruising the Aegean Sea, hopping around the various Greek Islands. This vacation met our bucket list expectations. It was magical and beautiful.

There, I got a tattoo to symbolize my healing journey to date. A visual expression of my narrative. My body, my choice. It reminds me that despite all odds, challenges, and difficulties I've faced, there lies the strength and power to overcome and thrive. My tattoo is prominently displayed on the nape of my neck. Most of the time, you cannot see it, as my hair covers this powerful symbol; however, when I pull up my hair, my voice is heard.

I selected a lotus flower to showcase the beauty of what can bloom from darkness. This flower grows in dark, muddy waters, and when it surfaces above the water, there is brightness and beauty.

My life story, I have discovered, is not as unique as I once believed. I share my story today to encourage others to experience their own transformations. It took me 44 years to remember what my brain so carefully archived all those years. There are missing parts and pieces of my life that either don't make sense or were sequestered deep in my brain. I am okay with that today. I know enough now. Understanding more about my family history and dynamics will help this all make more sense.

I have realized that my past is part of who I am today and that's also okay. I did not always feel that way, though. Many of us spend too much time hiding from our past, consciously or unconsciously. Running away allows for secrets and shame to cloud how we feel about ourselves and others.

I can only hypothesize that my running away from the past forced my brain to store painful recollections carefully. I always wondered why specific periods of my life appeared missing or foggy—and today, I know why. The brain is so powerful. It knows how and when to protect us.

Like the lotus flower, my life began in a challenging environment like those dark and murky waters, but eventually, I blossomed too. Many of our lives start that way, as life is a constant perpetuation of the hardships and struggles of our family's past. I know I am not alone. Our lineage does not determine who we will become, but it can set the stage for the future in many ways. Multi-generational cycles are natural and stubborn, but they can be broken.

My Mother - The Untold Story

To truly understand my mother, I journey back to the roots of her upbringing as narrated by her. Her story is a tapestry woven with threads of poverty, neglect, and unfulfilled dreams—a narrative that shaped the woman who would later become Mom.

Her early years were marked by financial hardship and struggle. Born into a family on the fringes of poverty, she learned the harsh realities of life at a tender age. The daily challenges of making ends meet left little room for the joys of childhood, as she and her five siblings often had to forgo necessities and simple pleasures.

My mother's upbringing was further complicated by a lack of proper nurturing and emotional support. Her parents were unable to provide the love, care, and guidance that she desperately needed as a child. Instead of a nurturing environment, my mother grew up in a family where self-reliance was valued over emotional expression.

Many days, my mother was required to stay home, care for the younger children, clean the house, and cook instead of going to school. Her story echoes Cinderella's tale. My mother loved school though. School was an escape and an opportunity to nourish her mind, body, and soul; however, education was never a priority in her family. She never graduated from high school.

Despite the absence of a formal education, my mother was resourceful, rich with practical knowledge and life skills. Hard work, determination, and a 'do it right the first time' mentality was instilled in her. Her desire to break free from the cycle of poverty was prevalent.

She decided at the age of 18 to leave that life behind. My mother envisioned a better life for herself with my biological father. She was naïve and hopeful for a brighter future. He was not the 'knight in shining armor' she had imagined. He was an alcoholic, a man who could not take care of his new family. We were young when my mother realized this marriage was far from the fairytale she had dreamed of. My brother was seven, I was five, and my sister was one when she left him. She was determined her children would have a better life than hers.

The ink was barely dry when my mother married my stepfather out of necessity. She was not in love. The cycle carried on.

Understanding my mother's background and challenges growing up has been instrumental in deepening my compassion and empathy towards her. I am starting to see beyond the rigid exterior shaped by her upbringing and to appreciate her strength and resilience, even though it was often hidden behind a facade of stoicism and unattainable expectations. My mother's story still lives on mysteriously to me, as details are missing and questions linger. Does she have secrets too? Or are the memories just too difficult to unravel at this point in her life? We probably have more in common than not.

"Don't Be Like Me"

If I had a dollar for every time I heard my mother say to me, *"Don't be like me,"* I would be a wealthy woman! As a young girl, I had no idea how those words would chase me through life like a bee, stinging me repeatedly. *"Finish school, Don't get pregnant young like I did, and never rely on a man to take care of you,"* were her commandments. Like mantras.

My independence grew at a very young age to make my mother proud. *"Don't be like me"* sounds harsh, but I knew it came from a place of love. It became part of me, much like the permanence of my tattoo.

Early on, I learned quickly that hugs, kisses, and words of encouragement were not handed out freely. It was hard to communicate with her. My mother's love language was through criticism and correction rather than physical touch or kind words. In her eyes, being too soft could create complacency; therefore, the absence of praise would push me to strive for excellence.

Watching my friends receive warm hugs from their mothers made me envious. Very rarely did my parents tell us children they loved us growing up, so I always sought love and acceptance from anyone who would give it to me. My stepfather, however, noticed my need for affection.

Constantly seeking approval and validation required me to suppress my needs and emotions to please others. Unconsciously, this is how I operated for most of my life. I was easily manipulated. Even though I did not want to do something, I did it anyway.

My sister and I had a strained relationship up until about two years ago. On her recent visit to Charlotte, I asked her, *"Why were we not close growing up?"* Her answer was shocking.

I remember her saying, *"Get off the stage, Kim!"* and I was offended, of course, as she implied I was putting on a performance. She continued, *"You were constantly trying to be in the limelight with Mom, Dad, and anyone else you could impress. I got so tired of watching you trying to suck up to Mom and hearing how great you were at everything."* We cried at my kitchen table, finally breaking through the wall that had been built around the two of us for the last 40 years.

It's tough to portray a life of positivity while experiencing negative self-talk. I know this feeling very well as an adult, so I can only imagine how I must have felt daily as a young girl. I was disappointed in myself for not getting straight A's, being too critical about my dance and cheer performances, and feeling like the 'ugly duckling' next to all the beautiful girls at school.

I was not happy with anything about myself. Every positive achievement was overshadowed by persistent negative internal chatter. I never learned to enjoy my wins—big or small.

While I am grateful for my mother's life lessons that made me strong, independent, and resilient, she had no idea I was suffocating from this relentless pursuit of excellence. I had developed an insatiable thirst for success. I wanted to be the best.

That persistent, nagging bee followed me and when I failed, I got stung. The fear of failure always prevailed, so I just worked harder and gave myself less grace and rest. Like my mother, I was determined to break the cycle and worked tirelessly to make sure I did not repeat history. I worked three jobs to support myself while obtaining my B.A. in Communications. And I persevered. I felt empowered for the first time in my life.

As I entered into my career after graduation, my thirst for success only grew stronger. Another promotion, bonuses, accolades, and awards adorned my walls over the next 30 years. My self-worth was dictated by my position, my ranking, and how much money I made. The work structure gave me a sense of normalcy, a map with the next steps, so I did not have to think about my inner turmoil. Success was my lifeline, and I occasionally heard that little voice telling me, *"You got this; you go, girl!"* But not as loud as the voice that would say, *"You won't make it, and you don't deserve this."* It was a strange dichotomy. I felt shame for winning and shame for 'losing'.

Meeting my first husband fed those negative inner voices more than ever. I married him three months after graduating from college. My mother tried to stop me. She saw herself in me when I said "yes". I settled for a man that took advantage of my kindness and love. Unfortunately, she was right.

He exploited my vulnerabilities, clouded my judgment, and slowly helped erode any self-worth I had left. We divorced after only four years of marriage. It is no surprise that I struggled with relationships as I did not see many, if any, positive examples of marriage or love in my life. I never had a father, either, just like Mom. My stepfather turned out to be a man I am ashamed to have called Dad most of my life.

I was unaware of my mother and stepfather's many issues. I did not realize the gravity of the situation with their marriage until about eight years ago. His words were a tangled web of half-truths and manipulations for over 40 years. His chauvinistic behavior made my mother look like a dutiful wife from the 1950s. He squandered every penny they had on other women without thinking about the consequences. He was a fraud. They were in financial turmoil. Still, she remained steadfast in her commitment to him.

His Ending, My Beginning

It was March 2020, the month and year that introduced isolation, loss, and death to many of our narratives. My stepfather was diagnosed with congestive heart failure a few years prior and was in and out of medical facilities. My mother and stepfather had separated while he was in the hospital. He had nowhere to go when it was time for his release.

My relationship with my stepfather started to deteriorate as the family uncovered more secrets about the 'other' life he was living. It was like a line of dominoes that kept falling one by one. Each day it was something new. An iPhone on my mother's Verizon bill that she was paying for belonging to another woman, an unregistered gun in his car, a personal loan he acquired for someone else, and phone calls from unknown bill collectors. It was like a Lifetime movie.

COVID was a blessing in disguise as I could not visit my stepfather at the hospital. The phone calls were awkward, and I just wished for him to call someone else. The call on this day was desperate. He always came to me when he needed something. He was a user I was learning, and typically, I always swooped in to help. This call was different, though. He no longer had a home.

I was incredibly angry with him that day on the phone. But my reaction went way beyond anger.. My mind and body were experiencing immense stress. Anxiety gripped me. My chest was heavy, like a weight sitting on me, and my hands trembled. It was a physical reaction responding to a hidden signal from the depths of my subconscious. I was paralyzed physically, mentally, and emotionally. My husband noticed my reaction, and just responded like he always did. He handled it. Mark was able to find an independent living facility that could take him. I remember the conversation went something like this – *"It's the right thing to do." We can't let him end up in a homeless shelter."*

My interactions with my stepfather after that phone call in April were minimal, as Mark continued to be my 'rock'. A few weeks before my stepfather died in May, he sent me a text requesting his Bible. I felt conflicted but willing to honor this request—an act of kindness to symbolize closure. I located the Bible and left it at the front desk. I wonder still today if he ever asked God for forgiveness for what he did to me.

When reflecting on my life, more often than not, I've felt mentally spent, exhausted, and overwhelmed. It's the type of exhaustion that chooses the couch over a walk, the type of overwhelming feeling that makes you not want to get up and face the world, and the type of mood that made my family wonder which of my faces they would see today. Historically, I never had a voice to ask for help when needed. I chose stress over joy, blame over forgiveness, anger over patience, and unhealthy food and alcohol over proper nourishment.

Back then, I was not present for my husband or children. My friends, co-workers, and extended family thought I was happy—and maybe I was on some days—but I was good at pretending. I did this my whole life. I was uncomfortable in my own body. I blamed COVID for a lot that year as this ugly virus had a sinister way of depleting our energy—mind, body, and soul. But it wasn't about COVID. My bucket was empty and needed to be filled.

My Awakening

"Trauma is personal. It does not disappear if it is not validated. When it is ignored or invalidated, the silent screams continue internally, heard only by the one held captive." - Danielle Bernock

I was still in my pajamas, snuggled with my favorite blanket on the couch and my husband Mark by my side. I convinced him it was the perfect day to binge-watch a 'chick flick' series with me. Firefly Lane had all the ingredients for an afternoon of mindless entertainment. This two-season series follows the friendship of Kate and Tully, sharing the ups and downs in their lives from their teenage years up until their 40s.

Netflix described this series as "fun, hilarious, and sassy". So I hit play, hoping to feel good.

We completed our streaming afternoon, and while I had hoped to feel more joy, my brain had a different idea. We continued to lounge on the couch, but I was struggling. My heart was heavy as I thought about Tully. As I watched her life unfold before me, I felt a familiar connection. She was just like me. She appeared happy and successful in all her endeavors, except for love. Tully hurt for many years because of one incident that changed her life forever.

In the show, she was raped at a high school party. I could not stop thinking about Tully. There was not enough time spent on how she felt when this happened and how it affected the rest of her life. But what did this have to do with me? *Everything.* I know this now but couldn't then.

Tully was alone with her secret. I felt myself relating to her as a woman and as a teenager. This fictitious character dominated my thoughts.

The room started to feel smaller, the walls closing in as a wave of unease washed over me. My heart raced, and my palms grew sweaty as fragmented memories began to surface. My heart and brain ran simultaneously. I was stuck on the couch, paralyzed by sensation. Then, the images. It felt like the paparazzi snapping one picture after another—quick flashes—images of me. As the brain slowed, the experience became more like those old-fashioned slide projectors, clicking loudly and slowly—one image after another.

I was sickened by the memories flashing before me. I questioned their validity. This memory dump continued for about 30 minutes in the presence of my husband—I did not say a word. My secret vault cracked open, breaking like a dam and filling up a bucket I did not want to be filled. My insides were knots, my muscles were tense, and my chest heavy. It was like a tidal wave of forgotten memories surging and flooding my consciousness.

Timelines were all over the place with missing details. None of it made logical sense to me. Memories of me as a young girl, teenager, and woman were dropping in. I wanted to look the other way, but I was forced to see it all. The images were unfathomable to me as a woman and a mother.

I saw images of me as a kid—playing with my Barbies, reading in my bedroom, and gathering clay from the creek and making pottery. These images were comforting and calmed the previous ones; however, I was not in charge and that was unsettling.

"He said it was normal, and I was his favorite...That he loved me."

I found myself alone with him in places he should never have been— my room, the bathroom, and even my parent's room while my mother was out of town for a few days.

I was six years old when he took me to the bathroom for the first time.

In my moment of anguish, the sobs were alternating with labored breaths. It was an emotional release accompanied by the struggle for air. I was sickened and saddened all at the same time. I could not speak. Mark felt helpless as my tears flowed without a clear explanation. My internal inquisition began.

"How could these memories have been repressed for 44 years?! Will Mark see me differently now? And who did he fall in love with? Would he understand this was not some forbidden secret I chose not to share?"

I was scared to hear what Mark was thinking. Sharing these haunting memories created additional weight and fear. I needed his love and acceptance as I revealed my brain's archives.

We got up and walked into the kitchen for water, where I collapsed onto the floor to shed my shame.

The words, *"My dad sexually abused me,"* sounded inaudible through the tears. The look on Mark's face was unforgettable. I shared my slideshow of memories with him the best I could.

"Why didn't you tell me before now?" he asked.

I said, *"I just remembered."* The conversation was humiliating. Why did I feel so dirty, like this was something I did?

When I shared that the memories started dropping in towards the end of Firefly Lane, he just listened. I told him I felt a closeness and connection with Tully. Her innocence was stolen, just like mine, and maybe I was triggered by watching her life story unfold before me. He held me like a child.

The remainder of the afternoon was a blur of insignificant chores to make time move faster. I wanted this day to be over, and so did Mark. I walked into our bedroom and found him lying on the bed, staring at the ceiling as if looking for guidance from above. The weeks that followed were tough for him. His pain turned to anger, and his anger was isolating. He looked at me with a sadness I had never seen before while being kind and supportive all at once. His hugs were abundant and long. *"There are no words for this type of pain,"* he said.

Imagine buying a puzzle, knowing there are missing pieces, and no picture of the puzzle on the box. My memories were just like this. They dropped in here and there, each piece hoping to find its place. The challenge, of course, was the absence of a clear picture. The months and weeks ahead had me frustrated trying to assemble it. I could only remember bits and pieces, and unfortunately, they swam around in my mind on and off all day. 44 years of 'stuff' stored away.

A few weeks after I shared my memories of that Saturday afternoon with my husband, I came home to find a picture of me hanging on a wall in our closet. I was three years old in my first dance recital costume. The little girl in the photo was so innocent and smiling so beautifully. She favored Shirley Temple with her perfect curls. I looked happy. My innocence had not been stolen yet. My husband wanted me to see the little girl I was before the abuse began. That little girl is still part of me. I say "Good morning" to her every day.

Embracing the Story

It has been four years since I figured out the "why behind the what". I have heard many times throughout my life, *"It will get worse before it gets better,"* and that was the case for me.

Anger, anxiety, and depression took a front seat position as time moved forward. Every nerve felt on edge, sending waves of panic throughout my body, making it feel like a medical emergency when it was just my body's response to heightened stress. I was in a constant state of 'fight or flight'. My mind and body felt under attack, and I had no idea how to fix it.

Mark and I were struggling with unresolved emotions. He chose silence as he was unsure what to say, and I chose silence as I was scared of what I might say. We had no idea this would take over our lives this way. My children were exceptionally resilient. Grant was 14 at the time, and Chase was eight years old. They often asked me, *"Are you not feeling well again, Mom?"* I usually responded with, *"Mommy is just tired."* It was the truth.

My desire to isolate myself eclipsed everything else. Mark handled what I could not. I had nothing left to give. I woke up, had coffee, made breakfast for the kids, showered, worked, and went home to my room—day after day. There was a gravitational pull to hide alone with these images swirling around in my head. And that I did.

Six months came and went.

Sadness and beauty converged one evening when Mark walked into my room and handed me his iPad. He found a therapist that specialized in sexual trauma. He said, *"Please call her."* A mix of gratitude and vulnerability swept over me. I knew it was time to get help.

Christina, my therapist, the last 3 years, along with my husband, pushed me forward. Getting help was a massive step and the beginning of my healing. I was sharing with a stranger, but I trusted her with my secrets.

I shared the 'surface' issues first. My wall was still fully intact. I told Christina I was depressed, anxious, and angry all the time, stressed about owning a new business, caring for my mother, and not feeling great about my performance as a mother and wife. And lastly, I told her my stepfather sexually abused me. I did it. I said it out loud.

I was never good at being vulnerable, but that was the day I started practicing. I met with her weekly. I still see her to safely peel back the layers—one at a time.

She Believed She Could, So She Did

When I told my mother, it had been nine months since that Saturday afternoon on the couch. I went through a period blaming her for what happened to me. *Why did she not notice anything? Why did she not protect me? Why did she marry him?*

She was almost stoic when I told her, talking more about her feelings instead of hugging me and apologizing for this insidious hell I was put through as a little girl. It was not the reaction I had hoped for. My relationship with my mother was strained for quite some time.

Fast-forward to six months ago. I was sitting in the parking lot of Trader Joe's when my mother called. She was curious to hear more about the story I was writing, but in reality, it was her turn to cry and share her truth. She said,

"After you left that day, I screamed at the top of my lungs! I was in so much pain that he did this to you. I am so sorry I did not handle that properly. I just did not know how."

We are better today. I respect my mother's fight to break the cycle. And she did—the best way she knew how. My sister and I are both happily married, raising our children with hugs and love. We have broken the cycle too.

I found my voice in 2021 when I shared my story with my therapist. Every word I write in my journal makes me feel lighter. I had baggage. It was time to unpack it. The more I shared, the more I started to realize how the shame of the abuse had followed me throughout my life—like my own personal shadow. It showed up in those negative inner voices. I was getting stronger, though. I was able to see a glimmer of joy in my life again.

The death of my stepfather was possibly the start of my awakening period before my memories were revealed. This man that was supposed to protect me. The man who promised he would take on the role of Dad when my biological father abandoned us. He stole my childhood away from me at the mere age of six. And as you can see, the death of an abuser does not bury the trauma. It still lives inside me, but it is tamed and nurtured.

The saying, "She believed she could so she did" has been following me around for four years now. When I was told "no" a couple of times by lenders to purchase the business we now own, I asked my husband to not give up. He kept pushing. I have a pin that was gifted to me and a picture in the window of my office that stares at me daily. As I write, I look down to my wrist and see my bracelet with this saying, as well. This thought process guided me—and continues to guide me—during dark days.

I assembled my puzzle. I am no longer searching for the missing pieces. I have accepted what I remember and not what I don't. My trauma is not my identity; however, I am who I am because of it. I am stronger today because I got help—the kind of help I did not know I needed until I watched Firefly Lane in 2020. I am a work in progress, but I am a strong, tenacious, and independent woman who is alive and thriving. These core values are embedded in me—part of my DNA.

No Light Without Darkness

I never thought I would say this but I am incredibly grateful I know what darkness looks like now. It would be harder to appreciate the light without seeing the dark. Just like the lotus flower, rising from the mud to bloom in beauty, we, too, can emerge from adversity—resilient and transformed. I finally found love—the real kind! My husband, Mark, and my children have been my rocks. I am eternally grateful to my family for supporting me through the storms.

I have been in sales and leadership for over 30 years, and it was always about being the best and winning. My bucket was filled when I received awards, accolades, promotions and when I bought my business. My career and entrepreneurial success guided me through life, much like the north star can do when you are lost. I am proud of what I have accomplished in spite of the adversity that made me so driven, but I don't need that anymore. I am no longer lost.

It's now 2024. I own a thriving commercial cleaning franchise in Charlotte, North Carolina. We help entrepreneurs start their businesses in the commercial cleaning sector. It's fast-paced, dynamic, and gratifying to teach individuals how to achieve their dream of business ownership.

My mentors with Women Thrive say *"Collaboration over competition".* That's where my heart is today—collaborating. I hope to help other women break their cycles sooner, share their stories quicker than I did, and empower women to find their voice and be kind to themselves.

Contributing to this book was never on my radar until a year ago. When my therapist asked me one day, *"What's next?"* I said, *"I don't know...maybe I will write a book."* Four days later, I stumbled upon Women Thrive on my business Facebook page. Nothing other than divine intervention.

"What's next?" My next chapter will reveal itself soon—I'm sure of it. Stay tuned.

Kim Blythe

Kim Blythe is a highly accomplished sales visionary, empowerment expert, business trailblazer, and author with over 30 years of experience in real estate and franchise sales. As the President of Jan Pro Franchise Development in the Charlotte, NC region Kim stands out for her professional acumen, tenacity, and winning persona emulating her true boss lady attitude. She is a passionate, authentic woman who loves hard and laughs often, embodying a unique blend of strength and warmth. Kim's career is a mosaic of triumphs and contributions to her field. She is known for her 'stage time' philosophy and "work hard, play hard culture" in her business. As a two-time winner of the Office of the Year and the prestigious Lifetime Achievement awards, Kim's relentless pursuit of excellence in sales, coaching and business has not gone unnoticed.

Kim's mission is two-fold; to diffuse the stigma that makes sexual trauma a taboo topic while helping women of all ages realize trauma is not a life sentence. "She believed she could, so she did" quote adorns her office as a daily reminder of Kim's mantra. Her plan to empower women to shed the secrets and shame associated with trauma have ignited a newfound passion to speak loudly from the rooftops and create her new title–Stigma Eradicator.

Kim has lived in Charlotte, NC, for the past 45 years and warmly embraces her southern roots. She finally found her true love later in life.

He is her best friend and business partner. Kim's greatest accomplishment is the blessing of her two boys Grant and Chase. Kim is also a stepmother, and her newest title, "Mimi," to two grandchildren. Feeling grateful every day for the opportunity to tell her story, Kim looks forward to sharing more about what life looks like on the other side of trauma-the brighter side.

https://linktr.ee/Kim.Blythe

3

FROM PRINCESS TO PAUPER

Diane Gilman

Beware!

E ven as a very young girl born in Los Angeles, I was obsessed with fashion. This made little sense, I didn't come from an artistic household, but rather a parental mentality scarred by escape from Nazi Germany. Middle-class conformity was the #1 priority in life.

We didn't have any fashion magazines in the house, but we did have plenty of Hollywood Photoplays. I loved to stare at the pages of movie stars dressed to lounge or glammed up for a night out on the town. I would fantasize that it was me designing their extravagant gowns. I was only four or five years old, but I already knew I wanted 'some of that'!

The years went by, but I never stopped dreaming. Then the '60s exploded and everything seemed possible. With a revolution in music, fashion, and politics, I began to meet music celebrities like Cher, Janis Joplin, Gracie Slick, Jimi Hendrix, and Rod Stewart. I would hand paint, jewel, embroider, rip and patch their own denim pieces. Each piece was an individual work of art. I began 'living the dream'. I loved it and I wanted more and more.

There is an ancient Chinese proverb that says, "Beware of what you wish for, you may get it."

All my life I had wished for fortune and fame. I got that dream, but never imagined the price I'd pay for it! Fast forward to New York City in the early 2000s. As my fashion business grew, I traveled incessantly for TV show appearances and often found myself returning home for only 12 hours before flying off again. I had a collection of pre-packed suitcases: One for a 4-day international trip, another for a 5-6 day stay in Florida (at QVC/Home Shopping Network), and an overnight bag for 1-day, dead-head trips like Toronto, Canada, for appearances on The Shopping Channel (TSC).

No, this was not the life of a jet setter, even though I flew First Class and stayed in five-star hotels. These trips were not luxury vacations. They were purely work and so performance driven.

My DG2 by Diane Gilman jeans have become an international fashion sensation - wowing London, Paris, Milan, Düsseldorf, Toronto and Sydney, Australia. I flew so frequently, Delta terminal at JFK airport was like the sitcom *Cheers* - everybody knew my name!

Sounds glam, right? On the surface, my 'runaway train' life was just that. But it is so true that 'All that glitters is not gold'. In reality, my life was lonely, gruelling, twenty-four-seven stress and expectations to perform. My design team always marvelled at how I would arrive in the office at 8 am for a long design day after flying in from a series of European shows just hours before. They would also wonder why I looked so angry and unhappy.

I felt worn out and sick a lot of the time, but I always rationalized that I was sleep-deprived, working on spare energy on top of jetlag. I was living the life of a thirty-year-old. No problem, except I was seventy-two years old.

Not only was I physically exhausted, but as the number one fashion personality in teleretail, my performance expectations were stratospheric. If I set a sales record, I was expected to break my own record in the next show. There was no resting on my laurels. Typically, I was expected to produce millions of dollars for every show visit. And I never wanted to disappoint. Tensions were high because big money was involved. The pressures piled up on a lifestyle with virtually no downtime. It was highly toxic!

In a strange twist of fate, I was trapped by my own success.

This was my own doing so I never dared complain. Besides, I had no choice. The major issue was no one would accept a substitute. I was the Chief Designer and my middle-aged fashion philosophy had built the brand. I alone could keep that going.

All the TV networks refused to broadcast any show without me. So there I was, commuting to Europe, averaging three round trips a month! On top of that, QVC/Home Shopping Network added shows and extra hours spontaneously. I felt like a doctor, I was always 'on call'.

Throughout all this activity, I refused to admit the ache in my left breast was getting more frequent and uncomfortable. There were small hard lumps right under the surface of my skin. "Simply calcium deposits," I told myself.

I was very good at compartmentalizing problems, so I wrapped the discomfort in a small, mental box and pushed it to the back of my consciousness.

I allowed myself, once in a while, to ponder how cruel 'karma' would be if this was breast cancer. At the height of my fame and success. I had waited so long and worked so hard to make my dreams come true, surely my fate was kinder than that.

Those thoughts were too terrifying to confront, and back into the compartment they went.

MERRY CHRISTMAS!

Unlike the rest of the professional workforce, holidays, and weekends for teleretailers like me were the most valuable. Holidays are the biggest sales shows of the year; everyone is home eating, drinking, relaxing and watching TV.

Easter, Memorial Day, 4th of July, Labor Day, Thanksgiving, and Christmas - these were prime airtime and I worked all of them! For nearly thirty years, I never had a slice of turkey or a present under the tree. I was setting sales records and chasing that 'number-one' crown constantly. Self-care has little place on the ladder to success.

This was not a lifestyle that nurtured friendships, or family, or camaraderie. Yet, triple-A personalities like mine - 'super-achievers' - are addicted to the competitive thrills. Thrills that are not only very addictive but potentially very destructive.

My self-care was relegated to the lowest priority. The business momentum pushed my life to the max. I never managed to carve out time to nurture or reboot or relish or enjoy.

Some days, the tensions were so overwhelming that I honestly felt like I was gulping poison. Delayed flights, design schedules, show expectations. The realization that you are only as good as your last show. It was a split screen. I loved the life I had worked so long and hard for, but I wasn't happy.

In mid-December 2017, the burning hard lump in my left breast that I'd ignored for over a year became an undeniable problem. I forced myself to see a gynaecologist friend for a breast exam. I could see the concerned look in his eyes as he examined me. He ordered me, with urgency, to get a sonogram. Despite this, I put the sonogram off until I'd wrapped my last shows of the year on Christmas Eve.

I literally got off a flight from my shows in Tampa, Florida, hopped into a car with my suitcase, and battled through rush-hour traffic to a Manhattan Diagnostic centre. I was travel weary, terrified, in denial, resentful and not at all happy to make this my first stop. The sonogram appeared uneventful, with bits of small talk but mostly silent. It went by rather quickly. But I was told to wait, afterwards. And no, I couldn't go home and get the results over the phone, as I had requested. I was just left sitting in a stuffy, dark room, barely the size of a broom cupboard, on Christmas Eve 2017, wearing a hospital gown, asking myself, "What am I doing here?" Honestly, I didn't have time for this nonsense.

~

Yet here I was, and I felt totally detached. I felt so sure I didn't belong here. There was no cancer in my family history, I had never even been in a hospital overnight.

The wait for someone to come and tell me anything was agonizing; 15 minutes became 30 minutes. Time crept by.

I was getting really impatient and about to get up, get dressed, and leave (escape) when a woman came rushing in.

She breathlessly blurted out, "I bet you wonder why you had to wait so long for your diagnosis. Well, it's because no one wanted to tell you. So I have to."

"Tell me what?"

"It's cancer. It's bad. It's everywhere. It's spread to both breasts. No mistake here.

It is hopeless."

I immediately went into an 'out of body' experience. I was present, but not. I felt like a distant observer hovering far above my physical form. My adrenaline level was off the charts. My ears were humming so loudly I could barely hear the words. My body was literally vibrating as I digested my death sentence.

I found it impossible to wrap my brain around the fact that my time on Earth was nearly done. I had so much left to do, but I'd heard the word "hopeless". No way out. No escape.

Cancer held a particular 'Doomsday' meaning for me. My life partner, Jim, had fought cancer for 10 years. I had been the primary caregiver and it truly broke my heart and spirit as I watched him suffer and slip away. His experience was forever burnt into my consciousness. So for me, cancer meant extreme physical pain, mental anguish, helplessness, and relentless decline.

Like a zombie, I got up, got dressed, and left to ponder my fate. And I began to make 'exit' plans over a holiday weekend that was meant for family warmth, indulgence, and good cheer.

But my world was forever changed. I had been plunged into darkness with an expiration date. This was an entirely new experience. I never knew I could feel so profoundly alone.

Merry Christmas!

"Just Call Me Elisa"

Somehow, I got home. My thoughts were chaotic, disjointed, and murky.

I am, under ordinary circumstances, a very pragmatic person. I like to plan out my life so I know where I'm headed. It seems to me I needed two plans — a survival plan and a dreaded exit plan. I was desolate. Being alone on Christmas Eve was nothing new. But being alone with myself in a big, silent home gave me no option but to face thoughts of mortality and admit I had done this to myself. The ultimate self-sabotage. It was not a good idea to go down that rabbit hole.

I am not a "coulda-woulda-shoulda" girl, so putting aside self-blame and regret for later, I silently settled on several immediate actionable goals, like calling the doctor who sent me to the clinic and letting him know the results. I hesitated as he had children and a wife. Who was I to dampen his Christmas?

Then, call my lawyer, review my will and notify my personal assistant. Whatever time I had left must be used efficiently. I was going to get control of myself. I would be in charge of me, no matter what!

So I did call the doctor, even though I really hated to bother him. He was, though, both a trusted health advisor and a friend. It was around 4 pm, deep twilight, and he picked up. I related that woman's words — especially the part about "hopeless" (which by the way, made me feel so worthless) and he said, "Don't be ridiculous, Diane! This is 2017, nothing is hopeless! I have to get off the call now."

I am thinking "Yes, of course. No one really cares about me and my fate."

Wrong!

"My family and I are sailing out of New York Harbor for the Caribbean. I have to call a dear friend of mine, Dr. Elisa Port, to take care of you before I lose cell range. You should expect a text from her shortly. Goodbye, and don't give up! Merry Christmas!" the doctor told me before hanging up.

Huge relief washed over me. Shortly after, Dr. Port, the leading breast cancer surgeon in America, texted me:

"Diane, meet me at 8:45 am, January 5th, at Mt. Sinai Hospital, Dubin Breast Cancer Clinic. Cannot say more. My plane is taking off for Marrakech!"

Another huge relief and serendipity. I had recently moved and my new home was just five blocks away from the hospital.

So, I settled in for the evening and had a serious talk with myself. I needed to stop 'floating' like an untethered balloon and get some practical direction. If I couldn't be 'fixed' what would be my legacy? And if I could get fixed, how would I weather the process?

I answered that self-imposed question on Christmas Day when I spontaneously called a good friend and talented writer, Jan Tuckwood, Senior Editor of The Palm Beach Post, to blurt out my proposition.

"Jan, I was just diagnosed with late-stage breast cancer. I want to co-author a book with you on my treatment pathway, no matter the results. This book may help thousands of women and will be my legacy. And oh, by the way, Merry Christmas!"

After a moment of shocked silence, Jan said yes!

Now, I could give structure and purpose to everything I was about to go through.

The days seemed endless but finally January 5th arrived. I filled out all the paperwork in a waiting room of very silent and sad women, like myself, and then was escorted into a diagnostic room. More interminable waiting and then the door popped open. In stepped a petite, middle-aged, blonde woman who introduced herself as Dr. Elisa Port, but insisted, "Just call me Elisa".

This was an extraordinary meeting. She looked me up and down and said, "Diane, you look like a perfectly healthy female with a localized disease in a part of your body you don't need if we have to take it away. And if that disease hasn't spread, you're one hundred percent curable. If it has spread, you are maintainable for years."

I was speechless but not for long. I kept asking, "Really? Curable? Really?" Until Elisa became annoyed.

"I don't have time for this repetition. Yes! One hundred percent curable! And by the way, women like you, Diane, always do best in treatment. You've worked your ass off all your life so you're used to knocking down obstacles. That will be your new job, saving your life. And I can tell, you are going to be great at it."

She had time to answer one final question - "Why? Why me?"

Answer: "CHRONIC STRESS! Your cancer is directly related to high levels of stress."

Oh my God! Fate had led me to the perfect cancer doctor. She spoke my language. She understood me. She put it all into a human scale I could handle.

Having Elisa on my team was as perfect as a perfectly terrible situation could be.

The Road to Needle Mountain

Now that I had a diagnosis and a plan: the strongest chemotherapy for the maximum amount of time my body could tolerate; then a double mastectomy; then hopefully breast replacement; and finally, radiation. I had to say my temporary goodbyes to everyone involved in my life. My business partners, who were panicked. My design team was scared and sad. And to QVC/Home Shopping Network TV executives and my loyal female audience.

None of these temporary uncouplings were easy and most were deeply stressful, but nothing compared to preparing, both physically and spiritually, for the dreaded chemo.

But first I had to fly to HSN for my *Goodbye For Now* shows. Afterwards, my TV team lined the hallways to say goodbye. My longtime model friends were crying and appeared agitated. I wanted calm support, a no-drama exit. But I got the exact opposite.

They followed me outside with a united plea, "Cancel chemo! Don't do chemo! Chemo is the killer!"

One insisted we drop to our knees on the rainy, wet parking lot pavement and pray the cancer away. "Just say no to chemo!"

Another insisted a green juice diet would conquer my disease. So "cancel chemo!" Finally begging me to fly to the Philippines for a "Manila Medicine Man" to "grab" the cancer out of my body without surgery.

What kind of karmic joke is this? What an insane way for the universe to test my faith, courage and resolve. It was so tempting but so deadly. I know my friends thought this was love, but they were killing me.

I wished with all my heart I could refuse chemo. But I couldn't. So I flew back to New York City the next morning and treatment began.

Twenty years before, I had watched my soulmate, Jim, endure round after round of poisonous chemicals. His suffering was monumental, and I was terrified. No, actually it was way beyond terror... I felt trapped. Like a caged animal. Either I faced up to my greatest fear, or I had little chance of surviving.

And now it was the night before the first infusion. I was alone and reflective.

I told myself this was not a dress rehearsal. This was the 'real deal'. Perhaps the greatest test of courage and faith I had ever faced. So I had better bring my A-game.

I was so wired into fear that surely this would be a restless, wide awake, unsettled night, but I was wrong. I fell right into a peaceful slumber and had an extraordinary dream. The kind of dream that is so hyper-real and delivers such a deep-soul message, it cannot be ignored or mistaken as either random or ordinary. And it will never be forgotten.

I must admit, I have had several of these extraordinary, spirit-sent dreams in my lifetime. Each one was so unique, so unforgettable, and so clearly a divine message at a time when I needed guidance.

In my dream, illogically, I was in my beloved 1963 VW Bug (the first car I ever had), driving down a rough, bumpy, gravel road with wilderness on both sides. I didn't know where I was or where I was going but I knew with a huge sense of urgency that I had to get to my destination. Suddenly, I screeched the car to an abrupt stop, where I faced a huge, vertical mountain that came out of nowhere. It came to a needlepoint at its top.

I couldn't get around it, couldn't climb it. And what would I do if I reached the razor-thin point on top? I just knew my very existence depended on getting to the other side. So, I backed up, gunned my engine and tried to drive up but just slid back down.

I tried several times and failed each attempt. I grew panicky realizing even if I reached the needle point peak, I would just crash down the other side. My distressed mind kept repeating "No way out! Now way out! No way out!"

Suddenly, in this all-too-real dream, I got out of my car, grew into a giant, and the needle mountain became nothing more than a sharp pebble under my feet to step over.

As I woke up and pondered the meaning of this vivid dream, the intended message was so clear: The only way to approach chemo or any of the terrifying and huge challenges life might have in store for us, is to become your own giant, rise above it, see it all from an aerial perspective, an overview. Deal with it and move on.

Jim used to say, "Better to be an eagle soaring above with miles of overview than to be an ant, overwhelmed by one blade of grass." This became my mantra, my key to successfully navigating not only the chemical assault about to begin but, quite frankly, any barrier the universe puts up to challenge me. This was a 'dream lesson' for life warriors!

And so began the battle for body and soul. Cancer doesn't discriminate!

LUCKY, LUCKY LUCKY!

One of the worst parts of the treatment was the infusion waiting room. Not that it wasn't beautiful, like much of the Dubin Center, but it was so sad. Many women would be holding their heads in their hands, weeping. The amount of fear was like a heavy fog.

We were all so different, but so much the same in our collective belief that cancer is a near-perfect enemy. No one is happy to have it in their body. I, myself, believed you had to have not only great medicine but also pure luck on your side to win this against-all-odds battle.

This was the first time in my adult life that I wasn't in an office, airplane, or TV studio working every day. Personal time was a novel concept. So I indulged myself by watching mountains of movies, especially one of my sci-fi favourites, *Alien*. I realized how much this movie's plot line and characters mirrored my current life. The alien, of course, was breast cancer, and I was Ripley, battling a relentless, ruthless, and all-powerful adversary. Surviving despite the odds, fearless and pragmatic. Cancer was a beast, like the alien - always adapting, always growing and getting stronger, and more lethal with each passing moment.

Every time I felt my faith slipping a bit, I watched that movie. Especially the last 15 minutes when she realizes she is trapped in a tiny space pod with the creature. She is terrified and keeps whispering to herself, "Lucky... Lucky... Lucky..."

I watched Ripley, a female warrior, make the very best out of the worst of situations, and so could I. A one-in-a-million chance? I'll take those odds! I will make it work for me.

The movie became a powerful metaphor of the enemy I had to conquer, the fight I had to win and my will to stay alive.

Then Came Sheila

It never occurred to me in my wildest dreams that I would ever look back on chemo with gratitude and respect, reverence and awe. I was at the height of my public recognition when I was diagnosed — straddling two of the vainest, most competitive glamour businesses in existence — fashion and television. Breast cancer had no place in this world. It was hardly an achievement I wanted to add to my resume.

~

At the time I entered treatment, I was the number one international fashion personality on teleretail with a fanbase of 650,000 women who live in my unique, middle-aged jeans!

My female customers crowned me 'The Queen of Jeans' and I was treated as royalty!

So, when I became a patient at Dubin Breast Cancer Clinic, I was sure I would receive priority celebrity treatment somehow. Oh my God — how delusional!

But, you see, I hadn't led a life of reality for a long time. I operated in a TV/fashion bubble of makeup artists, hairdressers, stylists, five-star hotels, first-class jets...

And actually, Dubin was perfect for carrying on my fantasy. Dubin was created by a woman, Dr. Eva Dubin, for women with a woman's disease. It had soft mellow furniture, rooms flooded with natural light, gorgeous views of Central Park, your own masseuse during treatment, fresh white orchids everywhere, private infusion rooms and beautifully catered lunches served during treatment. Oh, yes. There was no doubt in my mind that I had found my way to the perfect environment for my sick self. I was right at home amongst all these creature comforts.

Me being me, I honestly believed a bit of fame would convince cancer to ease up and give me a break, doctors would work harder for my cure, and nurses would bend over backwards to provide extra comfort. After all, I was a fashion icon and a beloved TV personality. Totally out of touch with reality... But then came Sheila.

Now, usually one of my friends would accompany me to chemo. No one wanted me to go through this alone, but this particular time, I was solo. If you asked me if this particular day contained the game-changing moment when I discovered a portal of understanding and enlightenment, gratitude, humility and soaring inspiration, I would have said, "Don't be stupid! It's just another treatment day, like any other.

Boy, was I ever wrong!

Well, it *began* as just another chemo day. But this particular day became a door I walked through to a shining future. I went into that infusion room as the 'old' Diane but left shiny and new.

And all because of Sheila - someone I had never met and knew nothing about, but I'm getting ahead of myself.

I was sitting in a private infusion room, with many needles in my arm, bored and scrolling through my phone. Like any good New York City fashionista, I 'dressed' for every chemo session - my Balenciaga sock sneakers, Gucci baseball cap, custom-made wig, cashmere sweats and Chanel tote bag, somehow believing good taste and designer accessories were going to save my life. Suddenly, I hear in the next room:

"SHEILA!"

"Hi! Oh, so glad you're here today!"

"Hey, everybody, Sheila is back!"

"Yeah! Come say hi!"

And just like that, literally every nurse came running into her room to say hello.

~

My first thoughts? Sheila must be a famous female news anchor, this being Manhattan, because everyone here knows her and wants to take care of her. Sheila must be famous and beautiful and rich and fabulous! In my warped mind, that's the only way you would get that sort of elevated VIP treatment. So my brain went into overdrive, painting a picture of Sheila... Luxuriant hair, glamorous designer clothes, the latest status handbag, attitude! Surely Sheila must be at the top of the 'food chain'.

I was jealous! I was incensed! Shelia's celebrity obviously outshone mine! How dare she? Didn't everybody know I was the 'Queen of Jeans'? So who was Sheila? The 'Countess of Chemo'!?

Then came the biggest insult to my ego of all — the nurses offered Sheila not one lunch but three of them at once. I was envious, slightly annoyed, and starving for gossip, so I called a nurse in and said: "Nurse, why didn't any of you offer me lunch today?"

The nurse replied, "Diane, you never eat lunch."

I replied, "That's true, but it would be nice to be asked, so dish, please! Who is Sheila? News anchor? Soap opera diva? Broadway star? and how come she takes multiple lunches? Who do you have to be around here to rate all that attention?"

The answer I was about to get stunned me and profoundly changed my life. The nurse looked at me oddly and said, "No, Diane! Sheila is a battered wife and mother forced to live in a homeless shelter because 'home' is too dangerous. She also happens to have stage 3 breast cancer, so imagine the difficulties of her current life. No privacy, no comfort. The food at the shelter is literally not edible so these extra lunches we offered her are not only her favourite but will be Sheila's only food for the next four days. Doesn't it just break your heart? She's such a lovely, sweet woman and her life is so rough. She has no money, no family, no home and no means to buy a good meal."

I was stunned. Ashamed. Humbled. So profoundly and deeply touched I could not speak! My eyes filled up with tears as I thought, "There but for the grace of God, go I." Everything I had believed in about self-worth and what truly mattered in life began to internally reorder itself after that. I began to understand my place in the universe. My path forward into wellness. My power. My voice. My purpose!

I came to appreciate my life gifts and think about how to use them on an elevated plane for a higher purpose. My path forward became my legacy — purposeful, intentional, spiritual and all about inspirational healing for others.

A miraculous change, you might say, from a brief encounter with Sheila — someone I never met, never even saw, never spoke a word to. Not on my radar as someone I admired by my shallow, judgmental standards. She was neither famous, nor rich, nor beautiful. She didn't have a closet bursting with frivolous designer clothes. She didn't have a mansion in the Hamptons, but what she represented taught me the most profound lesson of my adult life and set me on my current path to 'do good' and spread joy.

She did all that just by 'being Sheila'.

I have no idea whether Sheila survived or will ever read this and wonder if I'm talking about her. But I think of her often and wish her health and happiness. "Take care, Sheila, and know you are well-loved."

She will never know how powerful she was in changing a life (mine) and pushing it in a new direction - the right direction. Bravo, Sheila. You did for me, in just a couple of hours, what would have taken years of therapy. The life lessons I learnt from you are ingrained in my very be-ing: humility, compassion, empathy and community.

That silent goodbye to her was barely six years ago, and all the mem-ories of treatment pain, including a double mastectomy, have faded with time. My oncologist predicted this. She explained how our human brains do not have the capacity to hold extreme moments of pain. If you have gone through childbirth, you will know exactly what I mean. So true!

I will tell you the truth, at least my truth - I harbour no dark memories of breast cancer. None.

Miraculously, my clearest recollections are all uplifting moments of great insight, learning and soul expansion. Breast cancer cracked and peeled off a super defensive, crusty outer shell and I experienced an intense love of life and the 'wonder of it all' for perhaps the first time. I formed a new moral compass and a refreshed sense of purpose. And never, since that day, have I complained about even a minute of my life. No matter how difficult, I recognize the gift of life for the miracle it is. Every moment is sacred.

I don't think I would have ever stopped my toxic lifestyle if it hadn't been for a cancer diagnosis. I needed something so serious, so monumental, so profound, that it would stop me dead in my tracks. Otherwise, I would never have changed the trajectory of my life. Ironically, the disease that almost killed me actually saved my life.

And perhaps most importantly, I learnt there can be no light without darkness.

Coincidentally, I now have a new title. For some of my friends, I am no longer the "Queen Of Jeans" but have been renamed "The Lighthouse", because they observe that I try to spread light, joy, hope and empowerment to everyone around me. And once again, I am obsessed.

Princess to Pauper

As a cancer survivor, I would be remiss if I didn't remark on the cancer announcement Princess Kate gave on March 22nd, 2024. I was truly devastated. I never shed a tear for myself, but I wept for Kate.

How could this be? So young, beautiful, and privileged. Such a fairy tale existence.

From Princess to pauper, from future Queen of England to battered, homeless woman, cancer is the great equalizer.

I am humbled by the company I keep with my fellow 'life warriors'. We are forever connected by our common enemy.

Diane Gilman

Diane Gilman is a force to be reckoned with, reshaping the narrative of aging and challenging societal norms every step of the way. From her early days as a fashion rule-breaker to revolutionizing the industry with DG2 Jeans, she's proven that age is no barrier to success. At 78, Diane is just getting started on her third act, empowering women to embrace aging with confidence and vitality.

Her book, *Too Young To Be Old*, shares the electrifying story of her life and the empowering lessons she's learned along the way. From overcoming personal heartbreak to triumphing over breast cancer, Diane's journey is a testament to resilience and self-discovery. Through her podcast, *Too Young To Be Old with Diane Gilman*, she continues to inspire and educate the 50+ community on nutrition, health & wellness, beauty & skincare, fashion and aging solutions.

With her trademark lustrous white hair and fearless sense of style, Diane is a beacon of empowerment, urging women to define their own path and embrace their true selves. Join Diane in her mission to show the world how cool aging can be and discover the limitless possibilities that come with living your best life after 50.

https://thedianegilman.com/

4

ECHOES OF LOSS: BEYOND SHADOWS AND INTO LIGHT

Tajni Diller

L ife sure has its way of throwing curveballs, doesn't it? Just when you think you've got it all figured out, it can change in the blink of an eye. That's exactly what happened to me.

One particular summer morning, I had a list of errands to complete, and my simple, ordinary day would start with dropping off our tithe.

A friend shared a quote with me from the movie, Miss Peregrine's Home for Peculiar Children, that states, "I had just come to accept that my life would be ordinary when extraordinary things began to happen. The first of these came as a terrible shock and, like anything that changes you forever, split my life into halves: Before and After." And yes, what started that day as a simple task turned into a moment that split our lives into a "before" and "after".

I'm sharing this story because I know there are others out there, walking through storms, feeling lost in darkness and shadows. Maybe our stories aren't exactly the same, but my hope is to shine light into your dark places and dispel the shadows, to show that even in the darkest moments, you're not walking alone. Healing is a road marked with both setbacks and steps forward, but as you journey through it you will find moments of grace, moments that bring understanding, and eventually, a peace that settles in your soul.

It was a gorgeous August day, starting warm with a promise of at least ninety degrees. I had all three kids all buckled up in the SUV and we were off to get our weekly chores taken care of. My older two, Cody and Sara, were goofing around with their collection of toys and having sword fights in the third-row seat, and my littlest one, Luke, was snug in the middle seat. We headed out from our small town, passing a small corner market and then the chicken ranch, heading to our pastor's place a couple of towns over.

As I've already said, our first errand was to drop off our tithe (If you're unfamiliar with the term, the tithe is 10% of a household's annual earnings that is given in support of the Church). My husband, Dan, and I had decided to start tithing just that week. Coming up to a rural Stop sign, just a short mile from our destination, everything was good. I looked in the rearview window and was laughing at the kids' playfulness with each other. At ages 6 and 3, they were each other's best friends, and they didn't hold anything back when they were together. I did the usual look right, look left — no one coming, or so I thought. I pressed on the gas, and that's when our world turned upside down — literally. The impact was sudden and deafening and our SUV was instantly knocked on its side and spinning out of control. It was like time itself stopped, and all I could hear was the screeching of metal and shattering of glass. Then, just as quickly, everything went silent.

In the days following the accident, I can remember thinking in a very detached way how interesting it was that being knocked unconscious didn't hurt. It should hurt. I don't know how long I was unconscious in that vehicle, but I can tell you that coming out of being unconscious is terrifying. It felt like a rapid awakening on an adrenaline burst of terrified energy.

As I regained consciousness, strangers were yelling and trying to get my attention. My first thought was for my kids - I needed to know they were okay. The boys were scared and shaken but physically they seemed alright, thank God. But my daughter, my little girl, was trapped.

The sight of her, or rather, what I couldn't see of her, pinned in her seat, is something no parent should ever have to see.

My heart broke a million times at that moment. I gathered the boys to me, and while we waited for the arrival of the first responders, we prayed. As young as I was in my faith, my boys and I prayed the hardest, most genuine prayer I had ever prayed in my life. We prayed to God that He would do what was best for my little girl and He would give us the strength to accept that and to get through whatever came next.

Reflecting back on that whirlwind of confusion and chaos, it's difficult to clearly recall my own thoughts amid the shock and the hazy aftermath of being knocked unconscious. Time seemed distorted, as though the first responders, paramedics, life-flight helicopter, and tow truck converged all at once upon my regaining consciousness. Amid this turmoil, a compassionate stranger at the scene acted on my behalf to page Dan, providing him with the scant information available.

Upon receiving the call, Dan faced the agonizing drive of over two hours to the hospital, a journey fraught with uncertainty and dread. Each mile must have stretched endlessly as he grappled with the sparse details relayed by a voice he didn't recognize, telling him only that his family had been in a serious accident. The weight of not knowing the condition of his loved ones, coupled with the helplessness of the situation, likely burdened him with unbearable heaviness as he navigated the longest drive of his life, rushing towards answers he was not sure he wanted to hear.

Once the boys and I had been taken to the hospital and the boys had been tended and given the all-clear, Dan and I left to be with Sara. After being extricated from the wreckage and resuscitated at the scene of the accident, she had been life-flighted by helicopter to a different hospital and was now on life support. Our world quickly narrowed down to the beeps and hums of hospital machines. Three emotional days were spent in a blur of prayers, tears, and the incredible support of our friends and family. They rallied around us, ensuring our boys were cared for while we couldn't be there for them.

Walking into that hospital was like stepping onto another planet. Those nurses, though, were like rays of light in a very dark place, guiding us through each step, offering comfort when it seemed like the world was falling apart.

We quickly experienced a crash course in medical jargon and learned to interpret the mysterious readings on the life-support machines that seemed to dictate the rhythm of our hopes and fears. The constant fluctuations on the screen, which once seemed like cryptic codes, began to tell a story — and not one we wanted to hear. Medical terms the doctors were using, like "anoxia", a condition where the brain is deprived of oxygen, let us know more about the extent of trauma our daughter suffered in the accident.

Then came the conversations about organ donation. Navigating the heart-wrenching crossroads between hope for a full recovery and acceptance of what was increasingly looking like a devastating reality was an experience so unbelievable, it's hard to put into words. On one hand, we were clinging to any sliver of hope, desperately wanting our daughter to wake up, to return to us healthy and whole. Each beat of her heart, every breath she took, even if mechanically assisted, fueled this hope, kept it burning like a fragile flame in the darkness of our reality.

Yet, in the same breath, we found ourselves discussing organ donation. It felt like we were preparing to say goodbye to Sara, to let her go, even as every fiber of our being screamed in protest, yearning for a different outcome. The dichotomy of these conversations was jarring. Here we were, discussing the prospect of her giving life to others, while inside, everything felt like it was crumbling at the mere thought of losing her.

After three agonizing days filled with tests and tears, the doctors reached a heartrending conclusion. Sara had been without oxygen for too long at the accident scene, and despite their best efforts, the machines were now sustaining her body, with her brain showing no signs of responsiveness. With heavy hearts, we made the difficult decision to turn off the life support machines. In the midst of our profound sorrow, Sara's final gift was the gift of life to two other individuals. Each year, I find solace in praying for these two people, whose lives are even now still intertwined with ours in such a poignant way.

That drive home from the hospital without our daughter was one of the toughest things Dan or I have ever had to do. The car was so quiet, you could hear a pin drop, but it was like the silence was screaming at us. The feeling was completely surreal. Every mile we covered, every turn we took, it just hammered home the finality of it all.

Up until that moment, everything felt like a bad dream that I kept hoping we'd wake up from. But that drive - it was both the longest and shortest drive I've ever taken. The cloudy haze we'd been moving through at the hospital, with all its beeps and the comings and goings of nurses, suddenly gave way to a stark reality. We were heading home, a place that was supposed to be full of life and laughter, but now there would be a void. An emptiness where Sara's laughter and her personality should have been.

It was painful, so painfully real in that moment. We were leaving the hospital with one less member of our family, and there was no escaping that truth.

The following days and the day of the funeral are all a blur, and I have very few tangible memories of it. We scheduled it for late afternoon, the same day my oldest started first grade. I was determined that he would not miss his first day of the school year or be late because of the service. Looking back, I can see I was trying to control anything I could in a world that felt completely out of control.

After the funeral, our house was the gathering place for everyone who was mourning with us. It was comforting and overwhelming all at once. A friend of ours, practically family, insisted I start driving again and coerced me into a drive to the corner market and back. He knew, even if I didn't, that it was a step I needed to take towards healing.

It was during this time that I saw estranged family members talking for the first time in years. Grief has this way of cutting through the nonsense, reminding us of what's truly important. Those conversations, those small steps towards mending bridges, were memorable rays of light in a very dark time. It was also during this time that I began to desperately and intentionally deepen my walk with God. I didn't just hold steady with my faith where it was; it became the bedrock of my existence. In the immediate aftermath of losing Sara, my burgeoning faith was intertwined with a deep longing to one day be reunited with my daughter in Heaven. This longing was a light in the darkness, a promise of an eternal connection that transcended our earthly separation.

For Cody and Luke, the effects of their sister's passing impacted their daily lives, altering the dynamics of our family in both perceptible and imperceptible ways. Cody, so resilient in ways only a child can be, spoke of Sara and the accident with a quiet solemnity. It was clear, though, that beneath his words, a deep sadness had taken hold, dimming the vibrant energy he once radiated.

We watched, heartbroken yet proud, as he navigated his grief with a maturity beyond his six years. He continued to excel in school and maintained his friendships, which to Dan and me, seemed to be signs that he was finding his way. The decision to have him attend grief counseling came from a place of wanting to support him in every possible way, and when the counselor echoed our observations, affirming that he was processing his sister's absence in a healthy manner, it provided a small solace in the midst of our shared sorrow.

Our youngest felt Sara's absence in a raw, visceral way that tore at our hearts. At just 20 months old, his world had been changed by the loss of his favorite person. His cries for Sara were something we couldn't make right, and he couldn't understand why. All we could do was hold him, offer him our love and presence, and hope that with time, the sharpness of his distress would soften.

In these contrasting ways, our sons faced the void left by their sister. It was a season marked by tears, questions with no easy answers, and moments of unanswered longing. In many ways, as parents, witnessing their individual paths through grief was a test of our own strength.

Despite all that had happened, life didn't immediately hit the pause button for Dan and me. I became completely immersed in keeping life rolling for my family and Dan went back to work. I wasn't eating much, sleep was a stranger, and taking a moment to just grieve? I didn't even know how to begin to do that. I kept myself moving, always doing something, always making sure everyone was okay. I was on autopilot, ignoring my own needs, my own health. And not because I forgot to check in with myself, but because, somewhere inside, I felt like I didn't deserve that care or attention.

No one blamed me for what had happened; it was just an accident. But that didn't seem to matter to me. I was punishing myself. After many years and lots of reading and prayer, I have realized that I had all the markers for survivor's guilt. It is truly a heavy burden and a hard place to come back from. My heart breaks for those going through this type of depression and self-doubt.

It took me six weeks from the time of the accident — and constant nudging from my mom — to visit the doctor. Up until that point, I hadn't even been checked for injuries from the crash and due to my lack of self-care and nutrition, I was still sporting some pretty ugly bruises on my torso. But the real shocker came when the doctor told me that I was two months pregnant. In the midst of my self-imposed exile from self-care, this news was the catalyst that would bring me back to living life, and maybe the only thing that could have turned my trajectory around.

That doctor's visit marked a profound turning point in my journey of grief and healing. It wasn't just a routine check-up; it became the trigger that released so many emotions. The floodgates opened, and all the anger, sadness, and feelings of unfairness that I had been holding inside washed over me in waves of uncontrollable sobbing. It was a level of emotional release I hadn't experienced before in this season of mourning; a raw and unfiltered outpouring of everything I had been trying to hold together.

When I shared the news with Dan — that we were expecting again — he was stunned, and I can only imagine how I must have sounded over the phone as the words came out amidst tears and sobs, and likely sounding unhinged, as the weight of the revelation hit me. It wasn't merely about the shock of discovering a new life growing inside me; it was a stark wake-up call about my own health and well-being.

I realized in that moment how my coping mechanisms, or lack thereof, were not just affecting me. They had implications for this unexpected but precious new life, for our boys who needed their mother to be whole, for my husband who was sharing this journey of loss and now new life with me, and for myself. I understood that the path I was on wasn't sustainable and that this new life was a signal, a gift from God, prompting me to take better care of myself, find healthier ways to process my loss, and embrace the possibility of hope and healing — not just for me — but for our entire family. It was a transformative realization, marking the beginning of a new chapter in my journey through grief and towards healing.

As Dan and I hesitantly began sharing our news with friends and family, their reactions mirrored a spectrum of emotions. There were smiles, tears, and expressions of disbelief, as if our news was a plot twist in the collective story of our lives that no one had seen coming. Despite their own astonishment, their words and gestures were wrapped in kindness and encouragement, a testament to the strength of the bonds we shared with them. Sara's godmother's reaction still rings in my mind. She said, "I always see you with three kids, so it makes sense."

Those next seven months leading up to the birth of our youngest son, Marc, were a whirlwind. I thought we were doing okay, all things considered. Cody continued going about his days, diving into schoolwork and life with what I thought was resilience. But what we didn't realize was that he had completely repressed the memories of the accident. It was as if his mind had locked them away, too painful to confront. And that door stayed shut tight for ten years, until he was 16 years old, and attending an 'Every 15 Minutes' high school rally to raise awareness about drunk driving. That rally triggered his memories and that tightly shut door swung wide open. It was a shock to all of us, a delayed reaction that we never saw coming.

Then, there was Luke. Initially, he seemed to have escaped the accident unscathed. But just 10 weeks from the day we lost Sara, we were back in the hospital. This time with a diagnosis that felt like a cruel joke — at just 22 months old, his appendix had ruptured. The doctors were cautious, not wanting to give false hope. After tests and scans and physical exams, the doctors laid it out plainly: there was a 50% chance he wouldn't even make it through the surgery! Hearing this, coming only weeks after learning we were pregnant, and just months after burying our daughter, all of the fears came roaring back and overwhelmed my mind.

During those days and nights, I cried out to God with all of the raw emotion that was in me. I was brutally honest with Him in my prayers, in turn mad at Him for allowing all of these things to happen to my family, and thankful to Him for creating the path we needed to walk through this valley that we found ourselves in. He was gracious through it all and gave me the strength and confidence I needed to persevere. This time spent with the Lord in prayer helped forge in me a solid beginning of the faith that I rely on so quickly in my life now, and taught me that gentle, timid prayers are not what He is looking for.

As time passed, my faith continued to deepen. It evolved beyond a longing for reunion with my daughter; it became my lifeline, the very thing I clung to when everything else slipped through my fingers. In the uncertainty and the pain, my faith was unwavering, a source of comfort and strength in the dark when I had nowhere else to turn and no more tears to cry.

With a new baby on the way, my behavior and prayers took on a new dimension. I found myself eating not just out of necessity, but with a purpose — to nourish the life growing inside me. My prayers became more frequent, more fervent, each one a plea for a healthy child. And yes, I prayed with a specificity born from my experience — I prayed for a child who would not bear a striking resemblance to my daughter, a 'mini-me', not because I wanted to forget, but because I thought my heart needed a different path to healing.

I believed that if my new child were to look like Sara, then this new life would simply be a replacement of the one I lost and I didn't want that. I wanted a new child, a new relationship, a new personality, a new addition to our family, not a remake of what we'd already had. My prayers were specific; if we were given another girl, then we'd wish for her to have dark hair and green eyes, like my dad. A complete opposite to a sister she would never know.

Yet, when my new son was born, the Lord had answered my prayers in a different way. Marc looked just like her, just like me, truly a mirror image of the sister he would never meet. In that moment, I understood the power and the mystery of prayer in a way I never had before. My prayers were answered for a healthy child; not with the outcome I had envisioned, but with a profound lesson for me in acceptance that I don't always know what I need or what is best for me and the intricate ways in which faith can guide us.

My son's resemblance to my daughter is a bittersweet reminder of her, a beautiful thread connecting the past to the present, a sign that love, once given, never truly leaves us. It taught me that faith isn't just about the answers we receive, it's about how we carry those answers in our hearts — both the disappointing answers and the pleasing answers — how we find peace in the midst of hard questions, and how we learn to see the light of Jesus in even the most unexpected of places.

That year, the one I call 'our year of madness', changed me in ways I'm still unpacking. Before the accident, the thought of losing my children was something my brain had never contemplated. But after, oh after, it was as if fear had 'set up shop' in my head and wasn't planning on leaving anytime soon. It colored everything, every decision, every outing.

Simple errands like a run to the store became high-alert protection events, going to the park wasn't just a fun family outing anymore; it was a mission to keep my children safe. I was the mom always at the sidelines during practices, not because I was trying to be the ever-present helicopter parent, but because the thought of not being there, just in case something happened, was unbearable. Driving my kids to every field trip, volunteering for every school activity — not out of a desire for involvement, but out of a deep-seated fear of what might happen if I wasn't there — became my norm. My world had become this tightly wound sphere of 'what ifs', and every decision was filtered through this lens of fear and the need to protect my children.

This constant state of vigilance took its toll, not just on me but on my relationships as well. Friendships became strained as I navigated this new reality, my insecurities often misinterpreted as disinterest or aloofness. Commitments outside of my immediate family felt like monumental risks, as they could potentially limit my availability for my children. It was as if my entire identity had become wrapped up in preventing another tragedy, at the expense of almost everything else.

And then there was tithing. What was once an act of faith became a trigger, a reminder of the last normal day before our lives were turned upside down.

Fast forward a few more years of living like this and I experienced a life-changing realization. Suddenly, all the ways fear had been dictating my life came into sharp focus. I turned to prayer with a new intensity, looking for strength to overcome this pervasive fear and for wisdom to establish healthy boundaries. It wasn't just about me; it was about not wanting to smother my kids with my anxieties, about giving them the space to breathe, explore, and grow without the heavy blanket of my fears over them. About breaking generational curses, and not adding to them.

I yearned for freedom from fear, that genuine liberation from the anxiety and overwhelm that had oppressed me for so long. I wanted to fully trust in something greater than my own ability to protect and control. It was about leaning harder into my faith, trusting that it would guide me through the process of healing to find the balance I so desperately sought.

The victory wasn't instantaneous. Not even close. It's one thing to recognize the need for change and another to walk that path. Every prayer felt like a step forward, a movement towards a life where my decisions weren't made from a place of fear but from a place of intentionality.

Learning to develop healthy boundaries and putting them into action was a challenge. It meant giving my kids the freedom to make mistakes, to learn resilience, and to find their own strength. And for me, it was about finding peace in the uncertainty of life, embracing the beauty of letting go, and trusting that we were all going to be okay.

Breaking habits that had become such a part of me was a struggle. I had to pause in my reactions to everything I did daily and check where my response was coming from. If it was coming from a place of control, then I had to challenge myself and really think through my response and adjust it accordingly. Eventually, letting go became something that gave me peace. Accepting that, despite how hard I may try, I am ultimately not in control has given me true freedom. Learning my role, staying in my lane, accepting what I can and cannot control is more freeing than anything else I have experienced.

Today, tithing has become my declaration that my confidence doesn't lay in my own ability to navigate life's challenges, but in God's ability to guide, protect, and provide. No longer is it a reminder of that day now 30 years past and of the loss we faced. Instead, it has become a powerful statement of overcoming — overcoming fear, overcoming the trials and attacks life throws our way.

In times of reflection, I can't help but ponder the balance I've struck with my boys. Did I swing from holding them too close to perhaps stepping back too far? Did I overcompensate in giving them freedom, in my quest to not let fear dictate our lives? These questions linger, yet when I see the men they've become; strong, independent, and compassionate, I'm filled with a sense of peace.

Becoming 'Gran' to my oldest son's children has been a joy unlike any other. In their laughter, I hear echoes of the past but also the promise of the future. It's a role I cherish deeply, offering me a perspective on life's continuing cycle of renewal and hope.

Throughout it all, God's faithfulness has been my anchor. The blessings that have flowed, even from the deepest wounds, are a reminder of His unwavering presence. Establishing healthy boundaries was a turning point for me, a step towards reclaiming my life and my dreams. It allowed me to breathe, to look beyond survival, and to envision a future filled with possibilities.

As you close this chapter of my story, I invite you to reflect not only on the sorrows and struggles but on the strength and renewal that can emerge from them. If you find yourself navigating loss and trauma, know that you are not alone. The journey may feel overwhelming and full of shadows, but it also holds the promise of light — if we dare to reach for it.

I urge you to take active steps towards healing, just as I did. It begins with acknowledging your pain, allowing yourself to feel it fully, and then, slowly, finding the courage to move forward. Healing isn't linear or predictable; it twists and turns, but it always progresses.

Engage with your community, seek support from loved ones, or find solace in faith, as I did. Allow the stories of others, like the one you've just read, to carry you when your own light feels dim. Most importantly, be gentle with yourself during this process. Healing takes time, patience, and an immense amount of self-compassion.

Surprisingly, an impactful step is to consider how you might use your experience to help others. Whether through sharing your own story, offering a listening ear, or simply being present for someone in need. Your presence can be a powerful catalyst for healing — not just for yourself, but for others as well.

Let this be our collective call to action: to heal, to help, and to break the chains of generational curses for a hopeful tomorrow. Together, let's commit to this path of light, understanding that each step forward enriches not just our lives but also those of generations to come.

As I reflect on my journey, I am struck by the determination and strength it has taken to move from a place of unimaginable loss and trauma to one of healing and empowerment. My story, though unique in its details, shares common threads with many others who have faced significant challenges. I pray my experiences can offer hope and practical guidance for those navigating their own difficult paths. Healing is a deeply personal and ongoing process, requiring intentional effort and support from various sources. Whether you are just beginning your journey or continuing to work through it, the following questions are designed to help you apply the insights and strategies that have been instrumental in my own recovery. They aim to encourage self-reflection, promote proactive steps toward healing, and support your emotional well-being. As we end our time together, take a moment to ponder each question and consider how you can implement these ideas in your own life, fostering growth and strength in the face of adversity.

1. What are some steps you can take to forgive yourself and release any self-blame you may be carrying?
2. What signs of depression can you identify in yourself, and what strategies can you implement to manage it effectively?
3. Have you experienced a turning point that made you realize life continues after tragedy? How did it change your perspective?
4. How can your faith or belief system provide comfort and aid in your healing process?
5. What is the first step you need to take towards healing, and how can you motivate yourself to take it without overthinking?

Tajni Diller

Tajni's life story is one of determination and dedication. From becoming a wife and mother at 17 to establishing herself as a solopreneur by 25, she has navigated numerous roles with grace and determination. She completed her college education in her mid-40s, and around that same time she became a business owner, later becoming an employer and a pastor. Today, she is not only a Certified Tax Coach and Fractional CFO, but also the visionary founder of Boutique Books LLC, a revolutionary bookkeeping firm designed to empower small and medium-sized businesses. Her leadership extends into her community where she serves as a pastor and an international speaker, sharing her insights and inspiring others to overcome their financial challenges.

In her personal life, Tajni shares a deep and enduring partnership with her husband, Dan, to whom she's been married since 1988. They cherish their time with their three grown children and grandchildren, enjoying activities like camping, mountain explorations, bicycling, and road trips. This strong family foundation and shared values enrich Tajni's professional endeavours and her commitment to community service.

https://linktr.ee/tajnid

5

I AM HERE

LINDA CLARKE

"I'll just submerge myself in the ocean. Nobody will notice. Nobody will care that I'm gone. I just want to disappear."

That was the conversation I had with myself in August 2018. I stood at the shoreline of Goodman's Bay at 3:30 a.m. convinced that the only way to navigate what I was going through was to end my life. It was the quietest and darkest the beach had ever been. My car was the only one parked in the lot. That memory plays like a tape in my mind. The image was so clear.

How did I get here?

After four years of marriage, my husband announced that he felt it was time for us to separate. It was time for me and our son to find another place to live.

To the reader, anyone on your personal roller coaster: You are here. You matter.

I am humbled to share my story because I almost didn't make it. This is my testimony.

How did I get here?

I never confessed this to anyone. In fact, to this day, I cringe confessing it to myself. The morning after our wedding, I woke up and the first thought was, "I made a big mistake."

I never should have gotten married.

I swallowed that thought. After all, my husband wasn't a terrible person. This was the man who flew me to Paris, France, and proposed in a ferris wheel when I was five months pregnant. I figured it was just the jitters of being a new wife. I was anxious about moving to another city with our infant son. It was going to be okay.

Looking back, I'm not sure if 'okay' ever existed for me. We weren't miserable, but we definitely had disagreements. Court battles with my husband's oldest son's mother, living together as a family for the first time, our first Valentine's Day as a married couple.

We argued that evening right up to the moment we went for dinner because of a miscommunication on who was picking up his oldest son for a barber appointment. Looking at the photos from that night, no one could tell. We looked happy.

Months elapsed and the arguments got worse. I remember my iPad being thrown against the wall, followed by words that stung:

"Well, I bought it so I don't have to apologize or replace it."

Somehow, we made it to our first anniversary trip in Chicago. We sat down at this fancy restaurant in the city and our dinner discussion was a list of everything that I did wrong in our marriage. I vowed to never discuss this again. That night, I emotionally shut down in our marriage.

Nevertheless, we journeyed on. I call it a journey because when I look down at the Pandora bracelet my husband bought me after announcing I was pregnant, I see numbers. For every year of marriage, I received a charm with the number of years. It stopped at three.

Honestly, three was a push because I remember the Pandora box sitting on the dashboard of my car on my way to the office that morning. We had recently argued and I suppose it was awkward to present a gift at that moment.

Year Four. We moved in with my mother-in-law to save money for our own home. I never should have agreed to that move. I remember my mother's words that "there can only be one woman in the house". I'll never have peace in someone else's home.

A few weeks before our wedding anniversary, my husband surprised me with a European cruise with some close friends. I viewed this as a gesture that he wanted to salvage our marriage. We all got married the same year so it'd be a group anniversary party.

The cruise was phenomenal. I visited places I had never heard of. We went on adventures, took photos. Truly unforgettable.

On the second to last night of the cruise, I couldn't shake this feeling that something wasn't right. I didn't feel connected as a couple. I felt exhausted from putting on a show for our friends. There was no Year Four Pandora charm. It was more than the end of our vacation. It was the beginning of the end of our marriage.

The Crumbling

We returned from our cruise and the tension in our marriage was stifling. We continued making plans without communicating with each other. I will never forget that Saturday afternoon when our son had a medical emergency and had to be rushed to the doctor. We waited anxiously as the doctor ran tests. I was in a daze. The morning after, my husband calmly uttered the unthinkable:

"I think it's time for us to separate."

"How can you do this? We just left the doctor with our son."

"I was always planning to do this today. Our son does not control this family."

Days elapsed before I finally spoke. The shock of watching him move his things into our son's room was overwhelming. The first time I opened my mouth was in the driver's seat of my car, parked in front of my mother-in-law's house.

I called my best friend on the phone in my car (to ensure my son wouldn't hear) I screamed uncontrollably. I had no words. Just screams that sounded like they were coming from another body. She just sat on the phone and listened as I screamed years of frustration, pain and being overlooked. I was stunned and defeated.

The next morning was my fateful drive to the beach. The plan was to get in a training run for my first full marathon. I looked at that dark ocean and, in that moment, I felt like a failure. I failed as a wife. I failed as a mother. I didn't want to live with shame.

As I stepped onto the sand, something stopped me. I hadn't written a note because it wasn't my initial intent to take my own life. I realized I couldn't do that to my son. I couldn't live with the guilt of thinking that it was something he did or who he was that would make his mother leave him.

I walked away from the shore and, in the still of morning, ran laps around the park with tears rolling down my face. As the time passed and more people populated the park, I'm sure they thought I was crazy. Maybe I was.

I ran until fatigue overtook me. I came home to my son and began to face the reality of the two of us continuing this journey on our own. There was no way to explain this to a four-year-old child.

My husband drove us around for an apartment for me and our son. I thought, "who plans for this?" Nobody goes into a marriage thinking that you are on your own with a child looking for somewhere to go. The shame I felt was undeniable. I was struggling, holding on by a thread. I never told a soul. I spent my nights crying myself to sleep with my son next to me.

My Turning Point

I couldn't get a handle on the range of emotions I was experiencing. I knew that I needed to talk to someone other than my best friend. I needed someone trained in depression to help me. The person who came to mind was our marriage counselor. I figured, at best, she had some foundational knowledge of what was happening. She is an ordained minister. However, I had my concerns.

Would she secretly judge me? Convince me that God wanted me to work on my marriage?

I thought, "She is a woman and a mother. She could help me understand". Her message wasn't what God or the Bible says about divorce. She left me with a challenge:

"Whether you choose to stay or leave, you have to be okay - for you. Not for your spouse or your child."

My homework was to write a list of all of the goals, dreams, and aspirations that I had for my life. There was a catch - my list could not include anything about being a wife or a mother. This list was about being Linda.

I was stunned. I didn't know how to let my mind wander on who I could be without my family. Growing up, the lesson I learned in watching my parents was to just stick with it. You stay for your kids. Your happiness comes last.

Writing My Future

I did my homework. I went home and I wrote my list. I pushed away thoughts of "this is crazy," and "you don't have the strength to do this". The first thing on my list was easy to write because I had already begun the groundwork.

My marathon in Minneapolis was one month away. It was my first time traveling to a new city to compete in a race. I dreamt of my loved ones standing at the Finish line to embrace me. It dampened my spirit knowing this major milestone would be achieved on my own.

As I crossed the Finish line that afternoon, the race photographer snapped a photo of me washing away tears, both hands over my face. To a casual observer, those were the emotions of a first timer conquering her goal. For me? My mind had gone back to that dark morning in August on the beach and how I wasn't supposed to be where I am now.

Since that triumph, I took to heart the challenge that my counselor gave me. Running became my new passion. I spent my free time learning everything I could about the sport, completing two more full marathons in 2019. I traveled confidently, connecting with groups of runners across the United States.

In the fall of 2019, while on a training run with a friend preparing for the Detroit Free Press Marathon, I was asked to consider training people for distance running. I thought it was the craziest idea ever! I had just begun my journey as a distance runner! What could I offer anyone else? I am a mess. I am not good enough. I couldn't take on the responsibility of motivating another person. Cue those familiar thoughts.

I traveled to Detroit and ran my personal best time in the marathon. Enjoying my great marathon recovery period, I took an easy jog in the park when my phone rang. The caller's name was Karen and she had never competed in a race before in her life. However, when her employers placed a notice to compete in a 5K in January, she said yes. My friend, (coincidentally also named Karen), gave her my contact as a referral for run training.

She was terrified and seeking support. I paused before agreeing. But agree, I did. And, as they say, the rest is history. From there, Run Naturally was born.

Run Naturally: Inspire the Runner

January 1st, 2020, I birthed my second baby - my very own run coaching business. I didn't know all of the steps, but I was passionate about running and willing to learn the business aspects.

I enrolled in marketing and branding classes. I was a sponge, soaking up every drop of knowledge that I could get my hands on. When the COVID-19 pandemic hit, three months later, I pivoted and began virtual training sessions. It was a bump in the road, but I was committed to pushing forward.

When the United States Embassy launched its inaugural Academy for Women Entrepreneurs program in May 2020, I submitted my elevator pitch and was accepted. Months of workshops, sessions, and collaborations with like-minded women were exactly what I needed during the height of the pandemic.

I had the opportunity to present my business platform and win $5,000 of seed funding for my business. I advanced to the semi-final round. I became nervous in front of the panel and was ultimately unsuccessful in securing funding. I felt dejected about my underperformance during my 'Shark Tank' segment. The feeling of failure once again swelled in my chest.

Then, a colleague introduced me to another program called Toastmasters. I never imagined the impact this program would have on my life.

Toastmaster Linda Clarke

December 1st, 2020, I took the Toastmasters pledge and became a member. Still reeling over my business pitch months earlier, I figured this was an opportunity to learn how to present myself should I have another chance to pitch my business.

I didn't know how instrumental this program would be in helping me regain the strength and power of my voice.

I engaged myself in Toastmasters. It was something positive to do and focus my attention on as the pandemic worsened. I delivered my icebreaker speech in front of a room of strangers and felt pleased with my presentation.

Months into the program, depression resurfaced. It was over two years since my separation, with no resolution in sight. I wanted to work it out, yet my husband didn't want to talk about it. My mother was diagnosed with early signs of dementia. The grip of not having anyone to talk to paralyzed me.

That Tuesday, I delivered a speech entitled *I Am Not Your Superwoman*. It showed the entire audience my truth - that I was on the verge of an emotional breakdown.

I shook and let the tears flow at the lectern. I was tired of pretending to be strong. Nobody knew that I walked my son to his classroom every morning and sat in the parking lot opposite his school to cry before heading to work.

After my big disclosure, a woman - who later became my dear friend and mentor - tapped me and said:

"I don't know what you are going through, but you have a gift of telling your story. I'll see you at the next speech contest."

My stint in speech contests was short lived as I was on the fast track to leadership in Toastmasters. I wasn't telling my story on the contest stage, but I was speaking more than ever, gaining confidence, networking, recording podcasts - all of the things I had listed as goals two years earlier.

I wasn't comfortable disclosing I was separated. I kept it a secret, even from my family. After living apart for three years, I came to terms with the fact that our marriage was over.

Interestingly, my husband seemed comfortable with our living arrangement. One afternoon, he called asking for my opinion on where to send our son for summer camp. In classic fashion, more solemn words followed. This time they were my words:

"I think it's time to finalize our divorce."

Something in me clicked. I had enough. November 2021, we appeared in court to officially commence our proceedings. After court, I broke down in tears. I had no idea of the devastation I was about to face.

The Biggest Blow

In the midst of my divorce proceedings, my mother's health deteriorated. With everything I was going through, I didn't want to face losing her.

Late one night in February, I dreamt that my mother told me that she was going to leave me. I was so angry at her. How could she leave me? It was so vivid; I woke up with tears in my eyes.

I reached over and checked my phone. There was a message from my sister. My mother had been rushed to the hospital. My heart pounded in fear that my worst nightmare was coming true.

Weeks later, we received a call from the hospital. Mom's kids were all urged to come and visit her right away because the doctors weren't sure if she would make it. I hopped on the first flight back home to rush to the hospital to see my mom.

I want to believe that she knew I was there even in her unconscious state. She didn't leave us then. Days later, her doctors confirmed she was conscious and ready to be discharged. I worked remotely and prepared for my son and I to fly home and be with her once she was released.

I remember that Tuesday morning like it was yesterday. The weather was unusually cool. I remember running through the Cable Beach strip so effortlessly, it felt like I was flying. I ran my personal best 5K that morning. It was my last run before my trip.

As soon as I stepped in the door, my phone rang. My sister said she and my dad had been told to come to the hospital right away. The doctors didn't want to disclose information over the phone. I took a shower and when I stepped out, my sister called to tell me that our mother had passed away. It was March 29th at exactly 9:00 a.m.

My mind went blank. I called my friends. I called my mentors. There is no speech in the world that can prepare you to utter the words, "my mother passed away".

My friend Rosena drove me around New Providence, picked up my son and stopped for lunch. I watched everyone going about their normal routine while I felt like I was walking underwater. I fell asleep, later pitching up out of bed asking, "did I dream it?"

The next morning, I did the only thing that made sense to me. I went running. My feet pounded the pavement along the familiar stretch of Caves Beach, yet I never felt more lost. I dropped to the sand and cried, "Mummy, what am I supposed to do without you?"

For the second time in my adult life, I wanted to disappear. Lacking the energy to take my own life. I just wanted to lay down and die. I stopped eating. I couldn't sleep because I thought about my mother every minute. My friends were more than worried about me. They were afraid for me.

They watched me claw my way through my separation and they were not sure if I would survive losing my mom. To avoid my grief, I ran constantly. During one of my Saturday morning runs, I suffered a panic attack about two miles from my house. It was the closest thing to what I imagined a heart attack felt like. It left me terrified.

I barely remember the day we laid my mother to rest. I remember my older sister delivering her eulogy at the church. I remember her grave site. My son was at my left as I watched her casket being lowered. Screams emerged from my body that I don't think I ever heard before:

"Catch her!"

Those were the last words I heard before I fell to the ground. My son matched my screaming in that moment as I saw his godmothers rush to protect him. I don't know if my son screamed for his grandmother or because he thought he was losing his mother.

He was visibly shocked the entire day as I spent the afternoon assuring him that Mommy wasn't going anywhere. I was home with my family, I took the opportunity to complete my annual checkup. My doctor confirmed right before I boarded my flight that I wasn't well. I called my boss and decided to take a leave of absence from work.

The truth was that I hadn't been well for quite some time. I spent so much of my time - my life - surviving, hiding what I was going through. I realized that if I planned to find my way to wellness, I needed a leave of absence from many things.

It was time to focus on my mental health. I did the unthinkable. I took a leave of absence from competitive distance running and from

Run Naturally. My plan to return to Minneapolis for the Twin Cities Marathon in October halted.

The Way Forward

Taking the time off to attain wellness was not easy. In my season of grief and loss, I formed connections with people that proved to be toxic. It was time for me to release those connections. It was time to release habits that didn't add value.

I became very involved in Toastmasters. As I experienced growth and success in my public speaking and leadership journey, my moments at the lectern became therapeutic for me. I shared my tears, my grief, and my struggle. I shared my truth even as my voice shook and my hands trembled.

I refused to shrink. Instead, I spoke my truth. My innermost thoughts:

"Yes, I'm going through a divorce."

"What did he do? Was he cheating?"

It's amazing how people think you must endure the absolute worst before demanding better for your life.

My marriage failed. I am not a failure.

Part of my personal healing involved having my divorce finalized after four years of living apart. The irony is that as we co-parent, we maintain such a cordial relationship. We sit and have healthy conversations, finally. We host joint birthday celebrations for our son. I ask myself, "was it really necessary to endure so much hurt and pain to get here to this place?" I'm not sure that I'll ever know the answer, yet I continue to heal as I figure it out.

December 2022. It was the final meeting of the calendar year for one of my Toastmasters clubs. I delivered a speech about the impact of losing my mother in a way I never had before. Drawing on a line from the movie *The Color Purple*, my speech title was "I love you and I'm not dead". I watched my fellow members and guests sit with tears rolling down their faces. I cried as well. Once again, others wondered:

"When are you going to compete in the international speech contest?"

My story had a different message now.

Nine months had passed since I made the decision to take a break from marathon competition. Earlier that fall, the lottery ballot opened for the Chicago Marathon. The day before the ballot process closed, I submitted my application.

If my application was successful, I promised to run in the loving memory of my mother. December 5th, 2022, I received an email. I never read the email in its entirety. I only saw the word "Congratulations" and my tears flowed. At that moment. I realized that my passion was alive and that my mom would make sure that I would not live a defeated life. It was my mom saying to me:

"I love you and I'm not dead."

My Season of Excellence

January 1st, 2023: My word for the year was "excellence". My scripture verse for the year was 1 Corinthians 12:31: "Now eagerly desire the greater gifts. And yet, I will show you the most excellent way." That message for me meant that before I could see the best of what life has to offer, I must first de sire to do better. That was my foundation and motivation to curate a better life.

In January 2023, I attended my first TedX in Eustis, Florida, as a speaker-coach. In February, I visited Washington, D.C. for the first time. As an island girl, it was Christmas morning to see snow falling in person. I visited vineyards in the country, walked through art museums, took photos underneath the cherry blossoms.

I cry every Mother's Day. The first year without my mom, I almost didn't get out of bed. I wiped my eyes and had lunch at the marina with my son. He watches me cry and I now know that it's okay to say, "Mommy is feeling sad today because I miss my mother."

In Toastmasters, I spent my time speaking, mentoring, and motivating. I began applying for opportunities to speak on bigger stages and in front of bigger audiences. In May, I applied to be a speaker at our annual District Conference and my application was not selected. I felt dejected for weeks until I received an email, which I thought was a mistake. It was an invitation to deliver a Toast Talk at Toastmasters International Convention in the Bahamas in August.

Speaking on stage in front of thousands of people from all over the world proved to be the defining moment in the journey of the woman I was becoming. The woman who kept her story bottled up inside, was now speaking on the world stage. A month later, I was awarded my Distinguished Toastmasters Designation, the highest individual recognition in Toastmasters.

October 2023: Bank of America Chicago Marathon. In 45-degree windy conditions and a pulled calf muscle at Mile 13, I crossed 26.2 miles. Wearing a blue headband in recognition of dementia awareness, I fulfilled the promise I made to myself to honor the memory of my mother. I ran half of the race in pain, determined to not give up because she never did. Standing at the Finish line across from the Congress Hotel, the man who made me rediscover love waited and held my hand as I limped to the parking garage in tears. Five years ago, having that encouragement and support from someone I loved was merely a daydream.

There have been so many moments over the last six years where I felt invisible, incompetent, and incomplete. I fell to the ground, crawled, struggled to get back up and was knocked down even harder than before. I questioned who I was as a woman and a mother. I spent years berating myself because I couldn't keep my family together.

I never understood then how powerful that list would be for me all those years ago. Over time, I crossed items off the list and added more. I added titles to that list that I never dreamed of. As I added positive affirmations to my list, I removed the negative titles that I had etched in my memory.

My relationships failed. I am not a failure. Circumstances have left me feeling defeated. I am not defeated. I made the wrong choices. Everything I do isn't wrong. My mother left this earth. The values she instilled live within me.

I look down at my Pandora bracelet and smile now. No more are the charms denoting the number of years of a broken marriage. Today, there is a kaleidoscope of colors. Rose pink flowers. Silver hearts. Orange Mickey Mouse heads. Powder blue Chicago Marathon symbols. Red wine glasses. Bright pink footballs. My charms represent my new journey. They tell the story of the years I spent redefining who I am and what my happiness looks like.

To the woman reading this book with tears in her eyes thinking of how much you have lost, I have been where you are. I know what it is to think that the only way to find your peace is to shrink, to disappear. I know the pain of telling yourself that nobody will notice or care if you are here or not, to hear the person you love tell you that you are not good enough.

I know what it is to begin to find your footing in life only to be beat down with a devastating blow. You think that you will never recover. You believe you are incapable of being the mother that your innocent babies deserve. You may not even know who you are. You may not have a counselor or therapist to talk to yet. You may not know how to use your voice for anything but to cry or scream. If you are reading this chapter, reading this book, then I must believe that you, too, are desirous of something greater. I know you are.

Six years ago, I stood at the beach and tried to convince myself that nobody would miss me if I'm gone. That I would be just another statistic. I wouldn't matter. My purpose would remain unfulfilled.

The light I was meant to bring to this world may never have been seen. My impact may have never been felt. My voice may have never reached across lecterns and stages to ignite others. My message may have never been heard. I may never have been able to tell another woman that losing your marriage while raising your child is a big deal. Losing your mother while ending your marriage is a big deal. Holding your life together is a big deal. Navigating depression is a big deal. But I can say it to myself now. And I'm still here, to say it to you, too.

I thank God for every day I didn't make that decision. I am thankful that on that day I chose life - whatever that looked like at the time. I chose life with tears in my eyes. I chose life with pain in my heart. I chose life when I was grieving. I chose life when I was terrified. I chose life when I was sick.

On that day, I didn't disappear. Today, I am still here.

I Am Here.

Linda Clarke

Linda Clarke is a Real Estate Manager with an asset management company based in New Providence, The Bahamas. She has been a fixture in the financial services industry for twenty-five years including a stint in the Bahamas Government sector with the Ministry of Finance. She holds an LLM in International Finance and Banking Law from the University of Liverpool. She also holds an LLB (Hons) from the University of Huddersfield. Linda later obtained her Project Management Certification from the International Business Training Association. Linda's professional accolades include: Lean Six Sigma Practitioner designation, two-time Royal Performance winner for operational soundness and excellence, employee of the year and three-time top sales performer.

Linda became a member of Toastmasters International in December 2020. August 2023, she presented the 'Toast Talks' session at Toastmasters International Convention, sharing her six-week platform on inspiring confidence in public speaking at her workplace. Linda earned her Distinguished Toastmasters Designation, the highest individual award in Toastmasters in September 2023. She was recently elected Division B Director 2024-2025, with responsibility for twenty-two clubs in South Florida. Linda's long-term goal is establishing herself as a keynote speaker and mentor for women navigating motherhood, grief and depression. She shares her personal journey of parenting, divorce and the tragic loss of her mother in her book chapter.

Recreationally, Linda is a dedicated distance runner. She has competed in six full marathons and over seventy races in the Bahamas and across North America. She has coached and supported other women in training for distance races for two years using her platform, Run Naturally. Linda's new focus is serving at her church where her ten-year-old son is active in youth ministry. Linda plans to extend her passion for mentoring at her church with the LOVE ministry, aimed at mentoring teenage girls with college aspirations.

https://linktr.ee/lindaclarkespeaks

6

MY VOYAGE TO SELF-LOVE WHEN THE SUN RISES, EVERYTHING IS ILLUMINATED

Anna Berardi

"You have to die a few times before you can really live." - Charles Bukowski

There are mystical moments in life that change you forever. This was one of those moments. In 2012, I faced a metaphorical death, which turned out to be a profound rebirth. From trauma, burnout, and disease, I went through one hell of a storm. On the other side of the tempest, a sun was rising and illuminating a new authentic version of myself.

In May of that year, during a quiet evening, my doctor called me on the phone after reviewing my recent MRI results. "You are in the very early stage of a health condition called relapsing-remitting Multiple Sclerosis (RRMS)," he said. Then there was silence. A pause in the universe. Time stopped. *Pardon?* The air sucked out of the room. *What?* Gravity pulled me to the floor. At the age of 32, those words struck deep like a knife to the heart. *Why me?* That evening, I was alone in my flat in New York City. Paralyzed by fear. That one moment plunged me into an unwanted adventure I did not think I would survive.

Take a deep breath, Anna...Breathe...Lean into your meditation routines, the Buddhist mantra, Nam myo ho renge kyo, reconnect with your self-consciousness, spiritual power, vital force...The darker the night, the closer the dawn. You will find the way out of this nightmare...Breathe.

MS is an autoimmune disease; they say there is no cure. No hope for recovery. My doctor believed the only course of treatment was medication, therapy, and more drugs. I did not share that Western medical approach. Swallowing tablets every day meant giving my power away, along with side effects and fatigue. The intuitive choice for *me* was the Ayurveda path. My inner Buddhist faith chose healing through the connection of body and mind: personalized treatments with medicated oils, nourishing food, herbs, breathing, yoga.

"If you want to treat your disease with natural remedies, be assured you will use crutches to walk back to this hospital ten years from now." Those words coming from my physician still ring in my heart. Thankfully, I can't say the same for my body, which, over a decade later, has since run, danced, practiced yoga, climbed, and given birth to a precious baby girl.

Upon rejecting pills and choosing Ayurveda, my doctor sharply criticized me in front of my family, making me feel hopeless, and powerless. That moment made me question the emotional intelligence of Western medical education.

Determined, I fought with every fibre and cell of my body to reclaim my health and strength. Thanks to my grit and Buddhist practice, I have been able to turn obstacles in my path into opportunities.

My diagnosis has become a sweet reminder of how strong and courageous I am. How strong human bodies and minds are, and how we have power inside of us to direct our own healing. I am full of gratitude for taking the path I chose because I gained more than just a healed body. I am living authentically, fully present, and empowered. What a gift.

This girl is on fire - from Southern Italy to the world

One sensation remains vivid in my memory from my childhood: the blossoming lime trees and the Mediterranean sunlight caressing my cheeks under the endless sky of Apulia (Southern Italy). Childhood days in my rural town were spent exploring nature and overlooking the seaside. I always wanted to discover what was beyond the horizon; my innate curiosity became the foundation for a lifetime of exploration and self-discovery. Digger, my tiny blue pet racoon toy, was a beloved play-mate and good luck charm on my future voyages.

My admirable parents supported my thirst for knowledge by funding my studies. I wanted to make them proud and earn their love as a model student, seeking the best grades. At that time, I used to believe that I would only deserve love if I behaved like a good, caring girl. I embarked on a mission to become the best, most disciplined student. This marked the start of the perfectionism that later characterized my life. Success would prove my worth to the outer world, earning the admiration of others.

My perfectionism masked self-doubt and a fear of criticism. I grew up in a patriarchal Catholic region where women were expected to be always caring and submissive, like Madonnas. Although I was free and curious, at that time, this environment felt somehow disempowering for girls who couldn't be 100 percent themselves. No wonder it fed my self-doubt!

University life, far from that provincial environment, was a new world brimming with possibilities. I was driven to excel and please oth-ers. I kept myself busy with challenging classes, activities, and travel. Yet, I was restless. Deep inside, I felt a void. How could I fill my life with more excitement and passion, beyond getting top marks in my exams?

In 2000, I met Andrea, Stefania and Rita at University. We started to chant together the mantra "Nam myo ho renge kyo" and became pas-sionate about Japanese Soka Gakkai Buddhism. Founded by the Japa-nese priest, Nichiren Daishonin, in 1200, it is rooted in the teachings of the original Buddha, Shakyamuni (Siddharta Gautama). Keep in mind, I was raised as a devout Catholic at the Salesian nuns' school. By chant-ing, I was supposed to unlock inner wisdom, compassion, strength, and joy. Yet, instead of finding happiness, I heard my inner perfectionist and self-doubting voice that nagged, *Are you good enough or pretending?* That familiar, inescapable voice seeking external validation.

At first, Buddhist practice shook up my karmic tendencies and illuminated my limiting beliefs, including my inner critic. Obscurity always comes with the light. Yet, it was there, in 2001, that my old pattern of self-doubt began to shift bit by bit, day by day. Over time, chanting helped me to break through my limits and open up my life with courage and wisdom. It slowly transformed my inner critic into an inner guide.

After graduating with honors, I was hungry for life with excitement. Looking back, I can see I was greedy. I was never content with simplicity; I always wanted more than I needed.

At 24 years old, I packed up Digger and joined the UNAIDS Office in Honduras, ready for adventure on a new continent. An international career looked so fancy and full of social recognition. Just what I was craving! For the next decade, my life was a suitcase to be packed and unpacked, a frenetic "off you go". I fell in love with airports. Every flight was an adrenaline rush. I felt so brave and free.

～

In Honduras I loved my work - running advocacy campaigns, providing workshops about human rights, and empowering people living with HIV. I also helped found a local NGO (non-governmental organization), initiated by my Dutch friend, Mijke. My international career took me all the way to the UNICEF Regional Office in Panama and then to Jordan. Argentina, Peru, Nicaragua, Mexico: every new mission felt like a fresh breath, a wave of energy. *Look at me go!* I could become whoever I wanted in each country and felt fulfilled taking on each new challenge.

～

Amidst this whirlwind of missions, I maintained my Buddhist routine, as I was committed to my personal development. I chanted in the strangest places, for example in the middle of the Peruvian Amazon, or the Muslim mosques in Jordan. Surrounded by different cultures, languages, social classes and religions, those life experiences in the field deepened my appreciation of diversity.

Rushing towards each mission, I was thriving on the surface, but I was out of balance in terms of my yin and yang energies. In Chinese philosophy, yin and yang are the two opposite but complementary universal forces. Yin is the female, gentle, intuitive and nurturing power, while yang represents masculine action, ambition and strength. Immersed in tireless yang energy, I neglected my soft yin essence. I avoided long-term commitment in relationships because I was afraid of losing my freedom. My work kept me busy and made me feel seen, valued, and worthy.

New York City - the beauty of being perfectly imperfect

"One does not throw away gold because the bag that holds it is dirty; one does not ignore the sandalwood trees because of the foul odour of the Eranda trees around them; and one does not refuse to gather lotuses because the pond in the valley where they grow is not clean". Writings of Nichiren Daishonin WDN 1:38, "On Prayer" (pg.345).

My ambitious determination led me to NYC in 2012 to work at UNICEF Headquarters. *Cheers and go!* NYC was a dream come true. Walking the streets near Fifth Avenue, I felt like Julia Roberts in *Pretty Woman*, living the American dream. But success always comes with a price. My drive to succeed and my perfectionism reached new heights. I became a control freak workaholic, disassociated from life's small joys, and my self-care went out the window.

I was overworked in the pursuit of excellence. The vibrant energy of NYC's melting pot was thrilling, yet often left me feeling ungrounded and foggy. Mental hyperactivity, performance anxiety, and sensory overload marked my days. Mind, spirit, soul, and body became disconnected, and unbalanced.

~

The universe had plans to wake me from that "zombie" life.

First, my Italian partner ended our turbulent long-distance relationship. Abandoned and heartbroken, I was alone and lonely in the middle of skyscrapers. *Was my career really worth losing my love, back then?*

I buried my heartbreak in hard work. And then the universe spoke. One late afternoon, alone in the office, I was worried about a deadline the next day. All at once, I felt an electric sensation zip from my head all the way down my spine. *What was that? Did I just feel my body shaking me? Hmm...Anna, something is not right.*

~

My body was letting me know I was exhausted. I left the office and went home, something I rarely did. The next morning, I woke up with tingling in my left hand, which spread to my left leg and lumbar area. Insomnia, fatigue, and anxiety became my constant companions. Encouraged by fellow Buddhists, friends, and family, I sought medical help, and underwent tests and MRIs.

Just after finishing dinner one night, I received that phone call diagnosing me. The MRIs showed lesions on the nerve tissue in my back, that indicated the early stage of relapsing-remitting MS (RRMS).

Then, my life plunged into darkness. My physician only spoke of worsening symptoms and relapses, not a single word about recovery! I silently wondered: *Am I living a nightmare?* In a city with millions of people, I felt alone with no one to lean on. *What the hell am I doing here?*

~

In a state of confusion, misery, and panic, I hardly slept for a month after that phone call. I was frightened by that tingling sensation. My body was rebelling against me, desperately screaming, "No more hustle, baby! I can't take any more of your rushing."

I crashed. My relationship? Done. My health? Damaged. My arrogant ego? Winning.

My life split in two: before my doctor's phone call and after. Like an overwhelmed zombie, I continued on to the office. While doing my errands, I felt my left leg dragging numbly. The same leg that danced salsa in Latin America was now numb. I couldn't jump high during my Zumba classes at NYC's coolest gym. Every night before I went to bed, I prayed I would wake up healed, but the burning in my leg kept me from sleeping.

Then, the universe sent me an angel. Paola, a cheerful Italian colleague, helped me come out of my mental fog. She supported me in navigating the medical landscape: I was seeking the right holistic therapy like looking for water in the desert. One NYC Buddhist leader advised,

"Elevate your life condition so that it becomes higher than your disease. This struggle will make you who you truly are. Turn this moment into the greatest portal of your life, use it to create the most authentic version of yourself."

What, the portal of my life? I felt more like a prisoner in a dark tunnel. OK, Suffering is inevitable, but everything changes every minute. The lotus blossoms from the mud, the light dances with the shadow. Back to my inner guide through my chanting: to make room for more awareness, balance, direction.

As I looked for remedies, I continued to meet people who sparked rays of hope. A compassionate female neurologist gently inquired, "Do you wish to become a mother?" reassuring me that my diagnosis didn't make it impossible. This illuminated my lifelong dream of motherhood, the sunrise at the end of that dark tunnel. I envisioned a bright future. I owed it to myself and to my future family to regain my health.

Reiko, my Japanese shiatsu masseuse, was another beam of light. She used to say to me: "Do not blindly accept doctors' diagnoses. You can't possibly be ill because your eyes are so alive, bright, full of willpower. Nurture your inner light." This reminded me of the Apulian sunshine from my childhood.

The tingling in my left leg continued, and the more I stressed, the more it tingled. A bad cycle. I was in denial, pretending I was doing everything I could. Stubborn perfectionist that I was, I kept working and added Tai Chi and yoga at lunchtime, hoping for improvement. But nothing changed. The hamstring in my left leg remained damn tight. Interestingly, most of my symptoms were on the left side of my body, the feminine, yin part, which I was still neglecting.

⁓

I was angry with myself for getting sick just when I was set to thrive. Life, so tender and tough, can change in the flap of a butterfly's wings. From the summit of success to the bottom, from thriving to despair. I no longer felt like Pretty Woman, I felt like Broken Woman. I no longer knew who I was. Looking back now, I acknowledge the beauty of that imperfect moment. Fragility and vulnerability give life its beauty. The inner duality of suffering and blooming characterizes the impermanence of life, which gives us the opportunity for a new beginning and a new end.

I felt like a wildflower withstanding the harsh NYC wind. Then, one afternoon, in the chaos of my apartment, I came across an open page from the Writings of Nichiren Daishonin's Great Evil and Great Good: "Great events never have small omens. When great evil happens, great good follows." (p. 1119). Hope: evil is a springboard for growth, paving the way for the greater good. My inner guide intuitively knew that my current situation was not the final destination, so I kept moving forward.

After medical consultations, I realized that all I needed was one simple but rich thing: to be safely cocooned by my tribe. I packed up Digger and went home to Italy in August 2012, three months after my diagnosis. I landed softly in Apulia, soothed by my parents Biagio and Nuccia, and three siblings Angelo, Margherita and Giuseppe. *Grazie famiglia Berardi!*

My uncle, Dr. Michele, a few friends, and Buddhist faith companions were also very supportive at that time. Grounded in my motherland, I soaked up positive energy from my roots, from nature and the Mediterranean sunlight. The manic sensation in my left leg eased a little, but still let me know I was still not well. The warm tingling in my heart felt like healing was being summoned.

After two weeks, one thing was clear: my burnt-out body and mind were in need of rest and had no desire to return to NYC. I was trembling when I called my boss and told him I wasn't coming back. "We wish you a speedy recovery to happiness", that was the heartfelt message sent by my team in NYC with a red roses bouquet. *Thank you UNICEF colleagues for your support.* At 32, taking a career break felt like a giant leap into the unknown, but it was this bold action that shattered my pattern of perfectionism.

My health is worth more than any career. I am worthy of love and care. I can be seen, loved and valued, even if my career is on hold.

⁓

After my last hospital visit, I made myself two promises: 1) the next time I enter a hospital, it will be because I am pregnant and 2) self-respect and self-love are non-negotiable. I surrendered and welcomed an imperfect "slow living", focused on simple joys and self-care.

India - the art of balancing my yin & yang

"The darker the night, the closer the dawn. Victory in life is decided by that last concentrated burst of energy, filled with the determination to win." These words, written by my Buddhist mentor Daisaku Ikeda, reminded me to be tenacious during my healing journey.

The body has an incredible capacity to heal itself: each cell is replaced and regenerated every few weeks. Our immune system is meant to deal with intruders and toxins. I knew that if my health disorder was in me, I possessed that innate power to activate the healing in my body. I just had to find the right way to manifest it.

In September 2012, I flew to Germany to meet Dr. Prasanth Raghavan, an experienced Ayurvedic physician known for treating neurological disorders (including MS) at his accredited clinic, Ayush Prana. He delivered a sharp message: "You are mentally burned out and lovesick...If you do not prioritize your healing now, your incipient MS will progress."

~

I put my professional life on pause and embarked on a healing journey to Ayush Prana in Kerala, India. I committed to seven months of intensive treatment to rebalance my health. This was the bravest, most difficult decision of my life. It took guts! I was scared to jump into unknown territory, but I was excited to take on that new challenge; being in tune with nature, I knew my body needed a natural way to heal. I had a new mission that revitalized me.

After many years of hustling, I got a chance to pause and embrace the imperfect version of myself. Through that tingling sensation, my body, a sacred place, rescued me from my restless mode.

As the oldest form of Eastern medicine, Ayurveda (the science, "Veda," of preserving life, "Ayurv") teaches that beyond physical well-being, health is a radiant state of vitality achieved through body-mind balance and a harmonious lifestyle. This personalized, gentle approach to medicine focuses on treating the whole human being, eliminating impurities and increasing healthy resistance to disease.

In Kerala, I felt like I was waking up to life itself. I was pampered on the clinic grounds, surrounded by flowing rivers, birdsong, and the scent of jasmine. India was fascinating, vibrant, and full of contrasts -

similar to NYC. At that time, the clinic hosted 25 international young patients seeking relief from neurological conditions. We all led fast-paced lifestyles that left us physically unbalanced. I heard the same phrase over and over again: "I always wanted more." Each of us juggled a million things at the same time, disregarding the body-mind balance.

～

The initial treatment phase was tough. As my body went through a deep detoxifying process, I was physically weak, and sometimes, I felt lonely, pitying myself. At first, I wondered how unbalanced my constitution was: how would it get purified and for how long? Will this Ayurvedic treatment really be effective?

Nam myo ho renge kyo. With determination, anything is achievable. There is no room for doubt. I chose this path. My body can do this, it can be better. I'm still here to heal, to fight for that power back in my life. My dreams are waiting on the other side!

As I chanted, my inner guide felt the positive mindset returning. Daily treatment was a full-time commitment, disciplined and structured. Right after the roosters crowed, we started with sunrise breathing techniques, yoga, meditation, and the first medical treatment on an empty stomach. Then, consultations and other personalized treatments with herbal medications, and an anti-inflammatory diet. My body was immersed in streams of lukewarm medicated herbal oils to boost my immune system and stabilize my central nervous system. "Your state of mind should resemble a calm lake: serene and aligned," the doctor advised. I reduced mental hyperactivity, deepened my breathing, and rested well. I also dedicated myself to detaching from past stresses and fully focusing on making the most of my ongoing therapy.

There were colorful notes on my bathroom mirror, little positive reminders from me to myself: *This, too, shall pass. Embrace imperfections. Be mindful. Do not invite troubles at home. One day at the time, I'm going to get better and make it through this. Win no matter what.*

The Ayurvedic path showed me that nothing is lacking in nature; everything is perfectly balanced when we make space for the natural flow of prana (*life force*) through our cells. If we feed our cells with what they really need (physically, mentally, emotionally, and spiritually), they will regenerate and recover.

India was a perfect healing destination for me. During treatments and barefoot walks, I visualized each breath as a gentle yet powerful force, healing my tissues and lesions. I chanted to express gratitude for my ongoing recovery every morning. This act of self-care deeply shifted my mind, aligned with my body, soul, and spirit. I was creating a bounty of life force. I also envisioned motherhood when I wondered: *What if I could give birth and raise my child in full health?* Then, I felt my body trusting and getting better.

After the first year of treatment, the tingling sensation started to slowly fade. I became aware of what health looked and felt like. Prioritizing *my* needs became a powerful act of self-respect. I crafted a vision board with meaningful images about happiness and health: a peaceful mindset, physical workout, endorphins and serotonin, fulfilling work, spirituality, nature, wholesome diet, playfulness, uplifting relationships, honoring my intuition. I eventually used that vision board to reshape my new life with sustainable changes back home.

～

At the end of the treatment course, the Ayurvedic doctor congratulated me on my determination and positive attitude as they profoundly influenced my recovery. I was so proud of myself. I felt an energetic alignment. I could feel the power in my left leg again. It was the most beautiful feeling ever, like a newborn discovering new things! My lesions were smaller, tangible evidence of my healing progress. I knew that the Ayurvedic natural approach made the difference, as I never swallowed a single chemical pill.

～

Facing my illness was necessary to understand its hidden message. Now I realize I was just surviving in NYC, following my ego, and neglecting my true self. I was not aligned with my authentic expression, so the Universe forced me to rebuild. Ayurveda and Buddhist practice helped me replenish my energy, balance my yang and yin, and repair the cracks in a graceful way.

As my comfort companion through life's challenges, Digger meta-phorically transformed into the Indian Lord Ganesh, a symbol of wisdom, resilience, and grit to transmute adversity.

The rebirth - a Phoenix rising from the ashes

Back home in Italy in 2016, I found myself falling in love with life again. A new me and my health, the most profound treasure, were born again. I was in a hurry to explore and rebuild myself after India. This time, it was not yang energy driving me but a yin force.

The body does not heal alone but together with the emotions and mind that are trapped within it. With guidance from my therapist life coach, I journeyed back to confront my past traumas, acknowledge my childhood dynamics, stop numbing my feelings and tend to my inner adolescent with compassion. This newfound awareness, like an awakening, helped me to find my true voice beyond my limiting belief of self-doubt. My first post-treatment gift to myself was reaching back to my family as a renewed conscious person.

During the last few years, my inner voice has shifted from "I have to" or "I should" to "I get to", "I could", and "I want". Almost the opposite to perfectionism, I learned that good is good enough. In this society of having more and being perfect, I embrace my humanness. My sensitivity is no longer seen as a weakness, but as a core part of my intuitive yin essence, my guiding force.

I promised myself I would never again lose myself in the hustle and bustle. This meant no more greedy rush to the next novelty, be it a new partner or the next work adventure. No more people-pleasing masks and no more escaping.

I also promised myself to never lose the inner ability to connect with my body and to take care of it. I've almost overcome my fear of illness. Sometimes, when exhaustion sets in, I still experience a faint tingling in my lumbar area. It has become a gentle reminder from my body, a sage voice whispering: *You're overextending; please don't be so hard on yourself. Soften the frenetic yang rhythm and embrace your nurturing yin essence.*

As my body heals and I am able to find my voice, I celebrate my life's beauty with renewed joy every single day.

What are you grateful for? I am grateful for my earlier illness. With no major relapses in 12 years, I hold deep gratitude for my diagnosis, an unlikely ally that revealed a formidable strength within me. The sensation of freedom from my earlier diagnosis is bold. It no longer defines my identity. My illness has become the gateway to unlock my inner potential and upgrade my life. A legacy of growth.

From Maiden to Mother - Mompreneurship

"Mother, I do not think you are a delicate flower, a seedling so easily bruised. A dainty, breakable little thing. I think you are the root of the Tree of Life that holds the place together." Unknown

Post-treatment, I was hired by a foundation to craft a new educational programme on contemporary social issues for middle and high schools in Florence and Valencia. Meanwhile, I started teaching social studies part-time and pursued three yoga teacher certificates (hatha yoga, prenatal yoga, yoga for kids and youth). I became committed to kosen rufu, the Buddhist movement aiming to create value and peace in society. Volunteering at the Buddhist Cultural Centre in Florence, I took on a leadership role and empowered others to turn obstacles into opportunities, or in Buddhist slang, "karma into mission".

However, I still yearned to become a mother. I vowed to find a life partner with unconditional love, mutual respect, and a similar spiritual mindset. I wanted a noble heart on my side! *Make a vow, ask, and you shall receive!* In 2017, while volunteering at the Buddhist center, I met René. I saw a glimpse of home in his green eyes. His determination and integrity marked him out as the noble heart I was looking for.

During the C-19 pandemic, we moved together to a country house in the hills of Tuscany. There, our relationship blossomed. Like a firework or a shooting star, in August 2021, our pandemic baby arrived to make our world new once more. My daughter Isabel, the greatest gift of my new, healed life. During the natural birth, after the final push, I will never forget my scream of "Victory, I love you!" as I looked into her eyes. I had waited all my life for that precious moment.

Motherhood is profoundly revolutionizing my life (even on a cellular level). My "boss baby" (my daughter's nickname) is my engine for everything I do. Now, I write this story for her as she sleeps beside me. A written legacy for her future as an empowered woman. A second legacy I'm manifesting for her is to give her second name, Tomomi, to a heart-led holistic educational center I'm founding in the future. Tomomi is her Japanese name, given to her by our Buddhist mentor Ikeda: it means "the beauty of humankind". Inspired by my life journey, the holistic center will be aligned with the current Aquarian age and nurture kids and adults as whole mindful human beings: mind, body, and spirit. A safe, caring place to cultivate awareness, explore boundaries, and thrive.

I strive to be a social change-maker, creating an imperfect, but sustainable mompreneur life. A heart-centered life of value that is aligned with my body-mind holistic health, purpose, and family.

From now onwards - honoring my inner wealth

Karma is an evolutionary law of life, not a punitive one. We can turn storms into guiding winds.

Nowadays, my past struggles seem to make sense, and serve a greater purpose. I feel I have not only the privilege but also the responsibility to share my story with the world and help people find their best holistic health. My written healing story is a tribute to all people facing health challenges. It is my heartfelt wish that no one on this planet feels powerless when facing a diagnosis or any other adversity.

There is hope beyond the dance with our shadows. We are divinely conceived to heal and unleash our limitless ability to turn poison into medicine. The resilience and wisdom of the human body is unimaginable. After reading my story, I hope you feel empowered to direct your healing process rather than passively surrendering to illness. If I can touch and inspire even one reader who is struggling with health issues, I feel I have served my purpose and made an impact in this world.

A diagnosis doesn't have to be a life sentence and it does not define your human potential. It's our choice to take full responsibility for our lives, make conscious healthy choices and trust our bodies with patience. So we can rewrite the script of our diagnosis in a brighter way as a catalyst for greater life expansion.

My nonlinear journey is revealing a profound truth to me: health is absolute happiness, and happiness is our undeniable birthright. Beyond diagnoses, traumas, betrayals and failures, we all have that heart-rooted spark of joy. This society needs us in our most authentic, confident, and joyful place.

However, there are still days when I wonder what my life would have been like without my earlier diagnosis. Perhaps I would still be working in NYC. However, I know that without my MS - my incredible life ally - I would have lost the magic of this never-ending healing adventure. I would not have met all the past versions of me: the broken, career-oriented young woman; the wholehearted Buddhist believer; the tenacious Ayurvedic patient and yogi; the social studies teacher; the mindful mother. I have been my own experiment. Sometimes I long for my old adventurous life, but nowadays I feel more complete than ever and I honor each and every past version of me. They have led me to the current, authentic Anna as a heart-forward mompreneur.

Drawing on my childhood memories of Mediterranean sunlight, I commit to cultivating my inner sun, which represents our Buddhahood, that pure, enlightened nature that unites human potential with universal, infinite power, making the impossible possible. To unleash our inner sun, we must overcome our limiting beliefs, turning obstacles into opportunities. This alchemy reveals our inner wealth and affirms our inherent right to absolute happiness and health. Resolve to be the sun no matter what, for when it rises everything around it is illuminated and warmed.

As the Latins said: "Serva luce tuam." May you keep the light.

Anna Berardi

Anna is a dynamic and creative change-maker whose path has always been guided by her commitment to uplifting and serving the world with her gifts. A passionate human rights and social justice advocate and communicator, health mentor, yoga practitioner, mom, and author with over 20 years of professional experience working to make the world a better place. She holds two master's degrees - in international education and communications - and three yoga teaching certificates. With UNAIDS and UNICEF, she has defended the human rights of vulnerable kids and youth living with HIV across the globe. As an educator, she has crafted innovative social studies programmes for middle and high school students. From overcoming a major autoimmune disease to becoming a visionary entrepreneur and health coach, Anna is a zesty warrior at heart and a cycle breaker, embodying the spirit of resilient and positive, purpose-driven transformation.

Today, as a heart-led entrepreneur, Anna's mission is to mentor and coach people, especially young women and mothers, to ignite their innate limitless healing potential and embrace the beauty of being perfectly imperfect. With the motto 'We are medicine', Anna intuitively guides women to find their voice, embrace their mind-body awareness and manifest an optimal holistic health and thriving life. Thanks to her transformative mindset and lifestyle coaching strategies, women get to realise that an illness is not a life sentence but can become the catalyst for a greater life expansion.

Looking forward, as a mindful mother, she aims to create her own holistic educational center fostering a conscious, joyful living from the inside out. Being a lifelong wholehearted Buddhist, she has acted as the leader of the SGI
Buddhist Young Women's Division in her community. She enjoys her graceful life especially when she is teaching yoga to kids, traveling, cooking, dancing, soaking up the sun and nature, and cherishes moments with her family.

https://linktr.ee/anna.berardi

7

I AM STEPHANIE MYERS

STEPHANIE MYERS

"Every great dream begins with a dreamer. Always remember, you have within you the strength, the patience, and the passion to reach for the stars to change the world." Harriet Tubman

For many women, society has already determined what role a female should play among the genders. This places so many women at a disadvantage right from the start because millions of us are then reared by our parents, along with societal beliefs, regarding what jobs/roles are deemed acceptable for us to perform and which jobs we should not even consider. This dynamic plays heavily in our lives and how much we accept this 'training' depends on our inner beliefs about a woman's role at home and work. I am writing my piece of history in the spirit of love, kindness, and forgiveness.

Looking Within and Finding Me

From the beginning, I noticed something about me that was unlike others in my family. When I say family, I am also including aunts, uncles, cousins, and grandparents. My immediate family consisted of me, my brother and sister, and my mom and dad. I am the oldest of three kids. I felt what I can only describe as *different* growing up. I did not know exactly how or why I was different, but I got a certain feeling whenever I was around my family and words were spoken, facial expressions were given, that I had said something *different*. As long as my mother did not admonish me for what I had said, I thought nothing of their words or looks toward me. I was born in 1966. I can remember my father working at the shirt factory (one of the main jobs in my very small town in Tennessee).

My mother used to earn money from ironing clothes for other people until the day she went to work at the shirt factory too. Looking back, I can see how both my grandmothers were very subservient to their husbands. This was a time in which women just did as they were told and relied heavily on a man's paycheck for survival. At the time, I was too young to even notice how this norm would impact my life. All I wanted to do was go outside and play and then come inside for dinner and prepare for the next day.

Writing about my upbringing, I remember asking my mother, before she died in 2001, how her parents argued. What did she remember about her parents' disagreements and how did they handle them? She told me something that I had never considered before but made total sense. My mother said that my grandma never argued with my grandfather. Things were done exactly as he wanted them done. I then asked how Granny responded. Mom said she just held it in and never let her emotions show. I suppose by now I had felt so 'free' within myself that I never considered that restricted way of living for a woman. I mean, Granny was just 2 generations behind me...not 10 or 15 generations.

It's amazing how learning about your parents' lives (and the way they grew up) can shape the way a woman can look at and shape her own life. I now understand why my mother was such a fierce supporter of women. My mother never thought women were given the respect that we deserved nor regarded as equal members of society whose thoughts, values, and leadership capabilities were to be taken seriously. She hated that men seemingly made the decisions about everything important in life. I also know this stemmed from her own father's beliefs and then her husband's beliefs and treatment regarding women. Mom was *different* too, and such a determined woman. I remember her being thought of as 'bossy' and having a very no-nonsense approach to life.

This personality type actually drove many men and women insane because Mom's personality was often termed as being unladylike and not well suited to playing her role as a wife and mother.

I believe my mother simply did not want to merely be a wife and mother when she knew she could be so much more if only family and society would allow it. Just as women were trying to spread their wings and fly, the backlash was tremendous for those who dared to step out of formation and become the women they wanted to be. I remember asking my mother (I was in my forties when this question popped into my mind), "What did you want to be when you grew up?" The look on her face when she glanced over at me was a complete blank. It was like she had never considered the answer to that particular question. Not once. Not at all. I felt sorry for her at that moment.

After thinking hard for a couple of minutes, Mom finally said, "I suppose I would have chosen the military." I didn't press her, but I presumed my mother desired independence. To be allowed to prove her worth outside of motherhood or marriage. I have never considered what the military would have been like for a woman, let alone a Black woman in the mid1960s. I could see my mother as a warrior, though. I know when she married and had children, she was not being totally true to herself.

My mother's death has been the most tragic thing to happen in my life to this point. Once I learned to better manage her passing in my mind and deal with the reality of that, I was on my path to feeling unstoppable toward anything else that came my way.

People have asked me about the women who have inspired me to not settle for second-class citizenship; and make known to all how and why I feel women are an equal force to be reckoned with - just like a man. In answer to that question, my first inspiration is my mother, Mary Myers, because I saw the look of defeat on her face, and I never want to see that look on mine. Whether from a lack of resources, a lack of opportunity, or a lack of knowledge, my mother never lived the life she wanted...not even close. Second, is the woman who opened up my story, American abolitionist and social activist Harriet Tubman. To me, Harriet was the most hated and most hunted woman who fought for freedom. Against insurmountable odds, she overcame the impossible. The cherry on top is this remarkable General (who not only saved herself) led an army of people toward equality and freedom for all. Saying Harriet Tubman is an inspiration does not do justice to her name.

~

My father, on the other hand, was a very insecure man. While living in a rural southern town consisting mainly of white people, I was often told how he was talked down to as he shined shoes in the town square. The same town square where the Klu Klux Klan (KKK) held their rallies. Not all Black families fled to the North after the Civil War, many remained in the South. I found this interesting growing up because our town had about fifteen grownups who were Black and the rest of the town's population (maybe three thousand people?) were white. Did they need a KKK parade on the square in daylight for all to see and participate? Wasn't the majority of folks already supportive of the Klan and its beliefs anyway?

My dad did a stint in the Navy and while I heard a few racist stories about the military, for the most part, my family tried to shelter me and my siblings from all that was bad for Blacks in the South. I know they meant well but that was a mistake. My father needed to feel 'big' at home because society made him feel small. He needed my mother to be subservient. She refused. They divorced when I was 10 years old.

My father hated that I became a feminist. "You're acting like your mother," is all he would say to me. Instead of the quiet, non-opinionated teenager and young woman he had desired me to become, I was very outspoken and opinionated. He bought all of his children cars when they were each old enough to drive. All of his children except for me. That was my first face-to-face encounter with biased beliefs or what I refer to as warped thinking against women. It started at home. I loved my father, but I was not sorry that I disappointed him.

The Church

My parents seldom took us to church. Yes, if someone died, and of course, Easter and Christmas, but that was about it. My grandparents on both sides always made sure we were in church and knew about God. I often think that if it had not been for our grandparents, me and my siblings may have been atheists growing up instead of the Jesus-be-lieving people that we are today. I liked going to church as a kid. It was fun.

As I got older, however, the fun soon turned to boredom, and I quit going. I say it got boring (and it did) but I took issue with God preferring boys over girls and men over women. That is what the church taught me, anyway. Just be good and do as you are told; you are a girl soon to be a woman so get ready to play this role that is set up for you.

My grandmothers never spoke a word against this belief system. My grandpa, by this time my patriarchal grandfather had died, and our pas-tors definitely believed that women play a secondary role in the church and at home. Something in me did not agree. By now, I was attending church every blue moon like my parents. I am very *different* in my way of thinking and behaving than my parents ever thought. I'm okay with that.

Enough about the past though. Now is the time for a new beginning. A beginning that would transform me into the woman I am today.

I Shall Not Be Moved

I have worked many types of jobs in my 58 years. Many of these jobs were in male-dominated occupations. What I have learned during this time is that women are still striving for full gender equity at work, in business, and within society. I know things take time and I consider my-self a woman blessed with patience, but in this present moment, women may lose some of the rights regularly taken for granted. Rights that were fought for and won by others. Rights that we never once con-sidered losing until now. It is now that I feel the urge, no - the need - to do something about it.

～

As I mentioned earlier, I consider myself a patient woman up to a point. I never really know when or where that point ends, but I do give others a long runway to correct themselves should things go astray. It is in the spirit of patience that I have lived my life and tried not to make a fuss about circumstances unless absolutely necessary. Currently, I not only feel, but I *know* a 'fuss' has to be made regarding the biases women are told to endure. I have never accepted the status quo concerning what society, my family, or a church deemed appropriate for me.

I often feel as if tentacles are constricting around me attempting to squeeze the feminist, the gender equity activist, my authentic self, right out of me. All I want is to be free to make my own choices, free to show my leadership capabilities, and free to help others who may not know their way toward the light of freedom. I have a passion for waking up each morning and seeing women across the globe being true to who they are as women. No apologies or excuses are needed. I never wanted to feel like I had to choose 'this' way of living because 'that' way of living was unacceptable. Unacceptable to whom?

~

I feel life's freedoms are vanishing around me and my passion is to stretch out and free myself from biased attitudes. Over the years, I have experienced one-sided, distorted, or warped viewpoints when it came to me wanting and trying to be my true self. At first, I admit, I did not know if it was my being a woman or my being a Black woman that caused such prejudicial behavior to be directed toward me.

These revelatory statements or actions, mainly in work life, always made me stop and wonder what was happening and why it was happening. I mean, if you are nice and polite, do very good work, and continually strive to improve yourself, everybody should be okay with that, right? I have not been that fortunate. Yes, I have met numerous people and been to many places where everyone was treated fair, treated right.

Unfortunately, when some people felt the need to suffocate my hopes and dreams that turned what should have been a great time into a bad one. Now, I use my voice to speak up for myself and take action if necessary to receive the parity I deserve. Before I knew how to manage biased behavior and attitude, I'd use food to comfort myself whenever I was sad or feeling alone. Food wasn't allowing me to be the person that I knew I was meant to be. Plus, it made me fat! To make matters worse, I started experiencing headaches so bad that I had to see a neurologist. I believe it is true when doctors say stress can kill you!

~

I knew I had to get a grip on myself because I could feel my inner self slipping away. My soul was exhausted pretending to be what my family, my boss, coworkers, and societal norms thought I should be as a woman. This next statement will be unnerving for some of you: After gaining weight that I am still finding hard to shed after taking medication for frequent migraines, I made the decision to just be myself. I knew this decision would come with many attempted setbacks, a lot of speculation from others, and possible demotion up to and including firing from any job that I held. Was I willing to overcome fear? I was determined not to keep quiet any longer, and I was willing to take action if I needed to. I had to stop and think about where I was going to set the boundary line against fear. Yeah, fear. It had stopped me in the past but was I willing to let it stop me now?

My body was already rebelling against me by showing this was not the real me. My mind knew it too, even though I tried to convince myself that I did not have to speak up and sound the alarm whenever I was treated unfairly. I could no longer play along just to get along with others. Now what? Once my mind was made up - you know there is nothing like a woman with a made-up mind - I was determined to set a boundary line against harassing comments, unequal treatment, and other people's beliefs about me. I drew this line at home and work.

Work for the unequal treatment given for not being a member of the 'boys club' and home for allowing the disrespect of my feelings vs his needs. All this would STOP. A boundary line has now been drawn and has taken on more distinction and direction; it has transformed me into a woman who believes the best about myself and will politely address/correct anyone whose desire is to reduce me to what they believe a woman should be, do, act or think.

I do not want you to believe this process, this way of seeing myself and believing in myself, just happened overnight. It did not. I had to work up the courage to challenge and confront situations at work and home. One of the biggest enemies you have to overcome is yourself and your way of thinking and believing.

Mirror, Mirror on the wall...

There have been many gloomy days when my soul ached for something better. I would look in the mirror and think, "Who is this woman?" It was like people hearing you talk but not truly listening and understanding what you are saying to them. I thought and behaved exactly like I was supposed to for a young lady. Society demanded that I play my part, so I did.

By this time, my father had passed but my mother knew I had gone silent and gained weight. Seldom did I talk about work or my private life. People say all the time to talk and get it out, but I did not want to talk about how I felt my manager at work had passed me over for a promotion because I was a woman...or was it because I was Black? I wasn't quite sure. Sometimes racism and bias can seemingly walk hand-in-hand. I did not want to tell my mother, of all people, that my boyfriend needed me to play weak so he could be 'the man' and feel strong.

My mother became my best friend once I hit 30 and I still didn't want to share. My other best friend, Kim, was no help because I had seen her compromise her standards for every man she ever met, including the one she married. This was my problem, my cross to bear and I would figure it out. Figure it out I did!

I had to break the habit of falling in line regarding work, family, and society. I had to unlearn that being a no-nonsense woman was a bad thing. Often viewed as 'unladylike' if a situation called for me to be direct, confident, and clear when speaking to men, I would not hesitate to make my words plain. I have never viewed aggressiveness as a character flaw when I strive to go after a promotion or gain influence.

I have always been a go-getter and if there was something that I wanted, I worked hard or studied hard to get it. When an obstacle got in my way, as obstacles always do, I merely navigated in a direction that allowed me to go past it, around it, over it, or through it. Simple, right? No, not simple at all.

Most of the obstacles in my personal and professional life came from me deciding to use my voice; speaking up for what I knew was right and taking action if action was required. I have suffered many heartaches because I liked a man, but the man could not or refused to deal with a strong woman. Strong? I'm merely standing up for myself, so I do not get the short end of the stick. I spoke up at work because I refused to allow biased statements to just linger in the air without a response. I took action when biased attitudes prevented my promotion or shed a negative light on my character. Was I viewed by some as a trouble-maker? Yes, but I was true to myself and that felt great!

No one who knows me from both a personal or professional stand-point will tell you that I take things lying down. I love to compromise but everyone is not willing to compromise. I try to avoid conflict but sometimes conflict is what is called for. I come for peace, but many come for war...so war it is! Biases across the globe run rampant. Biases towards women are at an all-time high. My soul would feel strangulated if I could not seek the job I wanted, freely speak my peace without fear of intimidation, or use my mind to determine how I wanted to live my life. My passion is to live a fulfilling life. I am now on my way.

I do not have children nor have I ever been married. I can't say that I have regretted not having done either. After shedding the constraints that I placed on myself from my parents, church, and society, I now live a peaceful and grateful life. I am a blessed woman in that while life still has barriers that attempt to hold up and discourage me from obtaining my goals, I have the mental strength and fortitude to navigate and over-come those hurdles. I have been given the grace for such a time as this.

Please do not take this lightly; standing up for oneself and using your voice, not to mention taking some form of action if needed, is not some-thing that you do for fun. The backlash is real. I remember times when it seemed like everybody was against me, graffiti sprayed on my locker room door with very hostile words, my tire slashed or someone tam-pering with my lunch when kept in the department refrigerator.

On numerous occasions, romantic relationships that ended ages ago were now trying to use their influence and suggest that I could not make it without him in my life. I had to call the police and take out stalk-ing charges against two of them! Your life can descend into madness before getting better. Since I survived those ordeals, they now seem like nothing but at the time, I was afraid. I called upon my faith in Jesus and the belief within myself to see this through to the end. Did things get better? No, they got worse but I remained true to my beliefs. I held the line!

~

I can tell when what is happening in my life is about to change for the better. This is especially true when times are bad and lean toward getting worse. It is when my life hits rock bottom (or close to it) that a bounce back occurs. The prerequisite? I have to stick it out to the end. It is at the end, the bottom, that life takes a turn for good. I have witnessed this many times over and I know this to be true for me.

When the road is the darkest and I see no light at all or when people question me and ask if I know what I'm doing...this is when I know things are beginning to shift in my favor. First, it is easier to turn around and head back to the familiar when your life is in total darkness. If the ratio is one percent light and ninety-nine percent darkness, at least you see some light and even that feels better than no light at all.

When friends, family, and coworkers question your actions, often they are afraid for you. Remember that ole' saying "actions have consequences". When you stand up and represent yourself, they see in you something they do not possess within themselves: strength, determination, and a warrior spirit. Now I understand why millions are afraid of strong women. Mental strength moves the needle in life and proves that women can and will get things done decently and in order, usually the first time around. I had no other thought but to be me, the real me. The woman I am now and the woman I am becoming.

Difficult times that tested my soul eventually gave way to better times. Such is the ebb and flow of life. I had to stick to the plan and not look back at what was. I had to journey on to see what was in store for me when I was being real, true, authentic, you know the words. I shed many tears groping my way into the darkness trying to find something to hold onto and I found it. My faith was the anchor. I never would have endured if it was simply me believing in me. I tend to view life from a narrow lens. Combining the strength within myself with the unshakeable faith of the Almighty is what changed everything at work and home for the better. I would like to take all the credit, but I'd be lying to you if I did. Everyone needs an anchor when life's heaviest moments come our way. My anchor is God. Thank you, Jesus.

~

So, what is next in my life? Well, I build upon the foundation that is set. Do not think for one minute that my work or play environment comes free of biased thinking. I know how to uplift myself and I do not get as discouraged as I once did by people's limited beliefs regarding me. I write like it was so simple but when I think back to those times, I was so anxious just going to work and wondering what was going to be said or done. I remember going home and walking on eggshells, fearing an argument would break out over nothing.

Fear is torment and my mind, body, and soul does not like it. This is why I use my voice and, if necessary, take action to stop the limited beliefs and biased thinking directed toward me. This is a focus and a principle that I live by. I have learned over the years that if I do not think and act on my behalf, the dumbest person in the room will be telling me what to do when I know better! I may have a better way to operate, a better solution to a problem, a better way. Period. If I do not know, I will be the first to admit it but I refuse to play dumb or keep silent when I have a viable answer! Silence is no longer a strategy for me. I'm smart so why play dumb?

~

It has taken years for the Women's Movement to gain traction and give women some hope that our concerns mean something in the world. I realize true gender equity has not come full circle. Regrettably, I know some women believe we will never garner the respect and equality given to men. I can only represent my lot in life and share my lived experiences with you.

Moving from the past to the present day, my life is very fulfilling. I like the thought of girls and younger women being able to make decisions on their own as they mature; being strong enough emotionally to deal with any consequences that should come their way. Life truly boils down to what you believe about yourself. Those beliefs will determine if you are on the right track or not. As my mother always told me, "You don't have to believe me, life is the teacher, and you will learn from her." I understand that statement now more than ever. While I do believe we all harbor some sort of biased inclinations, I remain optimistic that, overall, those particular prejudices we have are not so extreme that they limit another person's dreams, stop someone from achieving their goals, or refuse to recognize another woman's accomplishments when she is worthy of honor and more money.

The biased tendencies of others make it extremely hard, if not impossible, to have a sense of belonging. Few people desire to be loners. I adore being part of a group that believes in, recognizes, and supports other people, especially women. I make no apologies for that. Have there been times when I questioned my judgment; should I take my manager to HR and report the biased issues I am experiencing from him/her? Yes. I question myself when I get afraid. Intimidation is real! Every time an incident happened at work or home, I questioned whether to stay at the job or leave the relationship. The optimist in me always sees the glass as half full even when it is near empty. What I want to say is this: Life is full of risks. Whether you leave or stay is up to the individual. I judge no one.

Life will teach you a lesson if you are paying attention and do as instructed. I do not want any woman to experience another person's warped viewpoint about us. It is women, along with those precious souls willing to stand with us, our allies, who make the fight for gender equity all the more important.

As I sit here and reflect on some of the more 'trying' times that made my soul ache, I do not tighten up or cringe. There are moments when I regret that I had to experience those times that set me on a course to confront and manage the ever-increasing biases that so many of us face today. While I judge no one, I frequently judge myself.

Instead of eating my emotions whenever I was frustrated, anxious, or depressed, I could have talked more openly and shared my experiences with people I trusted. Perhaps another perspective from a woman who had walked in my shoes beforehand could have offered some type of guidance. I don't know what every woman wants but I feel free to say that millions of women want the right to have a choice...a voice in any matter concerning them. I refuse to believe the majority of women desire for men to make all decisions concerning their lives for them if given a choice.

~

It would be remiss of me to leave out this one important aspect: the importance of sharing our stories. After reading my story, I hope you will feel uplifted and inspired to reach your full potential and higher self; gain the ability to speak your truth, and find your voice for gender equity and women's empowerment. Believe me, ladies, our revolution will be televised!

I'd love to hear from you! Contact me with any questions or concerns you may have at https://calendly.com/biasbreakingbeauty.

I am Stephanie Myers...now, who are you?

Stephanie Myers

Stephanie Myers aka Bias Breaking Beauty, is a seasoned advocate and change-maker with over two decades of experience working in male-dominated industries. Raised in an environment that often relegated women to second-class status, Stephanie was inspired by her mother, Mary, a resolute and competent woman who taught her to value her own strengths and individuality beyond societal expectations. This foundational belief fueled Stephanie's determination to alter the narrative for herself and other women striving to make their mark.

As an advocate for gender equity globally, Stephanie believes that exposing and challenging the biases women face is essential to the fight for gender equality. Her work serves as both a testimony and a guide, helping others recognize that women are capable of achieving anything they set their minds to and should be afforded the same privileges—recognition, compensation, and opportunities—that their male counterparts often receive.

Stephanie extends her advocacy through books, coaching, consultations, and speaking engagements designed to provoke thought, inspire action, and fuel movements toward gender equity. Her efforts are driven by a vision where the strength of one's character, rather than the gender assigned at birth, defines success. This clarion call for systemic change aims to empower women to assert their worth, demand their rightful place, and foster environments that value diversity and equity.

https://biasbreakingbeauty.com/

8

SORRY, I AM SORRY –
I DIDN'T KNOW HOW TO BE A MOM TO ME

GABS HAYES

A couple of years into marriage and two kids in tow, we proudly put the Under Contract sign in the construction dirt of our dream home. It was everything my husband dreamed of for our kids to grow up in, the perfect suburban neighborhood filled with large yards and plenty of families with kids the same age as ours. Quite the opposite of the childhoods we grew up in. Everything we thought dreams were made of.

While I was smiling on the outside about this massive milestone, the financial aspect of this house scared the living daylights out of me. It was the most grown-up thing we have ever done, and I was scared. But I wanted to support this dream because my husband painted the picture of community so well.

Two months later, I found out I was very unexpectedly pregnant with our third child. Suddenly that fear turned into pure thankfulness for this enormous house we were building to give the kids a stable space to grow up. When 'move in' day arrived, it brought this feeling of a whole new beginning.

It was the first time in my life I had ever built something from the ground up and lived in a brand-new house. While we couldn't afford to furnish all of it right away, it was ours and we were welcoming our babies into their 'forever home.' I can so vividly remember the day we handed them the keys as a 7 and 1-year-old to walk through the front door. It was the first time a space truly felt like ours because we picked every furnishing on the inside.

And just as soon as it was my happy place, it became my hell.

Adopting an Identity I Didn't Choose

Midway through my pregnancy, I went to the doctor for a regular checkup. I even told my husband he didn't need to come with me. My third time around, I knew the drill. I was going in for a quick check and then would go right back to work.

Except the universe wasn't in agreement with that plan. My life stopped right there in that exam room that day.

The words, "I am really sorry Mrs Hayes, but the baby no longer has a heartbeat" will forever be etched into my story as the time I stepped into a new identity, whether I was ready or not. The first real loss and grief journey in my life was a time that was unthinkable.

I lay on that ultrasound table in the presence of my doctor's team not even knowing how to process the thoughts that were racing through my mind. They had to remind me how to use the phone to even call my husband. And when he answered, there were no words to come out of my mouth. It was just sheer panic.

Avoiding hard conversations was characteristic of me. I would suffer in silence before I would speak up for my needs. I picked up this trait as a child who strived for external acceptance because I always lacked internal confidence. And here I was faced with the most difficult conversation of my life.

When I finally formulated words, through immense tears, I uttered, "The baby is dead, we have to go to the hospital."

Before I knew it, decisions about delivery were being made for me. I was being given instructions to go to the hospital to have my labour induced, and it all came flying at me faster than I could process. It was over before my mind even realized it had begun.

The delivery was extremely emotional. I begged the doctor to confirm one more time if my son was still alive. I cried "I'm not ready" when it was time to push. And I will never forget the serious tone of my doctor's voice when he told the nurse, "Get her to the operating room immediately."

Just after my precious baby entered this world, my body started to completely shut down. I required emergency surgery and a blood transfusion to save my life after the delivery.

Waking up from surgery, I was wheeled back into the delivery room to the most heartwarming and heartbreaking sight. My husband with our son had already gained his angel wings. This started our 24-hour countdown. Soaking up every precious hour we were given to spend with our son before he was sent to the crematory.

Unapologetically Saying Yes as a Survivor

After arriving home from the hospital, I went straight to my bed. Where I stayed for a week trying to process what in the world just happened to me and my world as I knew it.

I was flooded with more emotions and feelings than I had ever been taught to manage. It took me 2 weeks before I was able to pull the words together to tell my older children that we wouldn't have a new baby in the house. A lot of reciting over and over in my head combined with a few panicked Google searches of 'what to tell children when one of their siblings has died' helped me get out a few sentences that allowed them to begin healing on this grief journey with me.

Slowly, I was coming out of the fog. Still confused and heartbroken as ever but starting to see the clouds lift. I spent one more week acclimating myself back to life. Finding the strength to walk to the mailbox. Searching for the stability to face my neighbours and friends. One more week trying to figure out who I was after this life experience.

By week 4, I forced myself back to work because life kept going on around me, so I thought I had to keep going as well. The most isolating part of the grief journey continues to be that everyone's life goes on. Everyone is off to their normal daily activities while I am suddenly in bed because of a birthday or an anniversary that reminds me of my loss. These are the days when I don't have the words to explain why I feel this way, but everyone else has moved on and it feels like it's when the most explanation is needed. Plus, the fear of the bills of that expensive house came back with a vengeance.

My standard pattern of healing was direct and total avoidance of a situation, and then obsessive anxiety over the situation I had avoided. Compiled with this grief that I had never experienced in my life; I went all the way into obsessive anxiety. Obsessing over how to afford everything. Obsessing over how to feel normal again.

On my first day back, my boss took one look at me and sent me back home within my first 30 minutes in the office. They clearly saw what I had blinded myself to... I was not ready to return to 'normal'. I didn't even know what normal was. So, back on unpaid maternity leave, I went.

Those four weeks intended to help me heal felt like pure torture. I sat in the house alone during the day hearing phantom baby cries from a baby who wasn't there. To be in a silent house and hear what I swore were sounds of a baby crying sent my body and mind into a tailspin. My body started activating its caregiver nature, but the only person I had to take care of was me. My mind played the reality of my loss over and over, each and every time I swore I heard him cry.

For the first time in my life, I couldn't use avoidance to deal with a situation. There was nothing in this world that could preoccupy my emotions or my mind. It was me, my son's urn, and my depression... So, I did what I had never done before and decided it was time to face my pain instead of avoiding it. I had no idea what that looked like. I had no idea where to even start. But I was going to figure it out like everything else in my life.

I spent the next couple of years healing. Coming to terms with the fact that avoiding the healing process and distracting myself would only cause further harm in the future. I found a therapist who actually helped me see through the clouds of anxiety and depression with Cognitive Behavioral Therapy. I found a women's workout group in my neighbourhood and actually prioritized my physical health for once in my life. And I started to show up in the present.

I have been a Type A perfectionist for as far back as I can remember. I started reading the newspaper at the age of 4. I studied my way to acceptance in the gifted education program by 5th grade. I graduated high school a whole year early. I learned as a child that you are praised and rewarded for doing, not experiencing. So, it was my life's mission to always be crossing things off my to-do list.

And while this ability to have tunnel vision to do all the 'right' things in my life did bring me much success, it also meant my sole focus was always rushing to the next thing I should do to prove my success to others. And inadvertently I disassociated myself from the life right in front of me. I never learned how to be present in the moment because I was always thinking about tomorrow.

But I finally broke that cycle after committing to live my life to the fullest, experiencing all the things my son never would. I learned how to take care of myself. I learned how to prioritize my needs. And most importantly, I learned how to enjoy my life. From that point forward, I made decisions with a stark reminder that tomorrow isn't promised to any of us.

Within a year, I was coming back to life. I made friends in the neighbourhood and really started to feel like we were settling in our home. I had a very positive relationship with my health. As a family, we made a shared commitment to celebrate the little things and say yes to new experiences. Then an opportunity to make a big change in my career came, and I jumped in full force.

It was a chance to start over, where the baggage of my grief didn't come with me. Or so I thought.

Apparently, Trauma Relapses are a Thing

If you have walked your own grief journey, you know the ups and downs. The 'I'm doing so great' and then the 'grief just hit me out of nowhere' moments can at times be only mere minutes apart. Over the first year in my new role, the 'I'm doing great' part of my grief journey continued.

Until we made the decision to add one more little one to the family. I was initially so ecstatic to become a mom of four. But before I knew it, I became filled with this mental anguish that no one prepared me for when having a baby after loss. Waking up scared every single day. Walking through life in a constant state of worry. Carrying a doppler monitor with me everywhere I go to reassure myself that everything is okay once I hear the baby's heartbeat.

My doctors had me on extreme limitations because of how high-risk I was, and that only added to my constant fear. I stopped working out. I stopped travelling. I became a hermit when I wasn't working or at one of my kids' activities. Before I even realized it, I reverted back to doing instead of resting, doing to alleviate my fears with money, and doing to avoid my feelings. Seeking solace in these familiar, albeit destructive, behaviours.

The healing progress I made seemed to vanish. The lingering trauma I buried after my son's passing resurfaced, and I began a path of destructive avoidance.

I went back to work 4 weeks after my daughter was born, just as the Covid-19 lockdown started because I couldn't sit at home and deal with the wild range of postpartum feelings. Feeling so relieved she was here safely and feeling so angry that my son wasn't. So thankful that my husband was home with us and so confused at what the pandemic lockdown even was. In my best attempt to avoid the duality of emotions, I got back to work to be in my safe space.

Since work was fully remote, I justified my choice to cut my maternity leave short because we were all home anyway. My husband was laid off due to the pandemic. I had support at home with the kids. I might as well go back to collecting my full paycheck.

Plus, I finally had everything I wanted in my career. I found my dream job, a tech startup where I was seen as the expert and the strategic leader. It felt like the perfect place to be my safe space. Until I ran myself into the ground. Spiralling out of control and reaching an emotional overload and point of no return.

If only I knew then what I know now, I would realize I blamed it all on my job. Yet I was the real culprit of burning myself out.

I told myself the story of work being the bad guy. They were expecting too much out of me. They were demanding I was available 24/7. They were killing me on the inside. I completely justified my desire to quit. And I ultimately handed in my resignation letter to my dreams because I was still blaming everyone else for my actions.

Looking back, this was the first sign that I had more work to do. Because the reality is, I set all of those expectations on myself. I failed to set boundaries with me. I was trying to define my joy and my worth by working 80-hour weeks. I walked out of my office with the most picturesque view of the city on the 23rd floor for the last time. And what I thought was going to be the 'solve' to all of my problems, was just the beginning of years of chaos forcing me to finally hit rock bottom in my life. Even though on the outside I had it all.

But of course, I didn't realize that! Being stubborn I thrived on being a control freak. I continued this path of avoidance and making rash decisions for a few more years in an emotional breakdown after my daughter was born.

That dream house, where my kids were so happy, I convinced my husband it wasn't right for us and it was time to sell it. I packed them up and moved them halfway across the country to a city we had never even visited before. I started another job, loved so many aspects of it, then justified quitting because I still was not self-aware of my own triggers. Borrowed $50k and put our family in a financially rough spot to renovate the new house as an attempt to make my kids feel the comfort of the home they were forced to leave. And spent a lot of time convincing everyone that I was so freaking happy!

In reality, so many things about our fresh start in a new town I really was happy about. But the other truth is, my inability to face my trauma head-on cost me and my family. Our dreams, our stability, and trust in my decision-making capabilities. It undid all of my recovery and healing from years prior. It made me so jaded at the world around me. Jealousy, anger, anxiety... you name almost any emotion on the uncomfortable side of the emotion wheel, I was experiencing it. It led me to a vicious cycle of decisions that made my life so much harder. Because I wasn't living in my full truth, and I had not learned to fully take care of myself.

The universe has a powerful way of shaking us to wake up. We are put on this earth to live full lives. To be joyful. To make memories. And to leave an impact. But in order to do that, we have to fully see that power in ourselves. The universe decided it was time for another major wake-up call.

Nothing Could Prepare Me for This Wakeup Call

We were a little over one year into getting settled in our new town. We loved our home. We were making incredible friends that felt so aligned to the family life we were creating. We spent more time together as a family than we had in 11 years of having kids. And I fully stepped into entrepreneurship, launching a consulting business.

Things finally felt like they were coming together. I was satisfied with life and had no real desire to run away or make big changes. We had friends and family flying out to visit us and they all could feel how much we were enjoying this chapter of our life.

I felt safe to explore new versions of myself. I started seeing an acupuncturist. I hired a life coach and a business coach. I bought a bike and would commute via bike when I could. Our house became the kids' hang-out house in our neighbourhood, and my kids were getting exposure to things I never thought possible - Future CEO camps, nature schooling, and making a difference in their community. Things felt pretty great, but I had two dark clouds looming over me that I was not ready to address.

I created new relationships that were very authentic to the person I was becoming, but I hadn't figured out how to authentically show up in my former relationships - including those with the people living in the house with me.

And the biggest struggling relationship of them all... my relationship with money. I was scared of money. I was scared of managing it. I was scared of facing it. I was scared of never having enough of it.

I started to recognize this, but things were going so good I just swept them under the rug. Facing them meant I may go back into a depressive, irrational state, so I became complacent. Being the sole financial manager of our family, I convinced myself it was okay to constantly shuffle money from bank account to bank account to make ends meet. I believed I was okay with the work-life balance grind of being able to do it all, for everyone BUT me.

Until I couldn't be complacent anymore.

Just before Mother's Day, I faced the stark reminder that tomorrow isn't promised to any of us. And being complacent was blocking me from showing up fully every day.

The end of a beautiful week was upon us. Our best friends from our old neighbourhood spent a week with us in our new town. We did all the things! We explored, we ate well, we hung out, and the kids played until their hearts were content. But on Friday morning, my youngest woke up with another asthma battle.

Ever since we moved to our new town, her asthma and allergies were off the chart. Anytime she got a cold, she landed in the hospital for a few days to get her oxygen levels back up. She had this audible grunt every time she was starting to have trouble breathing, so when she woke up that morning with her grunting sounds... I jumped into action. Nebulizer, allergy medicine, and a steamy shower. Doing everything we had been taught to at home to reopen her lungs to try and keep her out of the hospital.

But this time was different. As I got in the shower with her, she had a seizure and she left me.

With the most guttural scream, I yelled for help and just kept screaming to call 911. My husband took her lifeless body out of my arms and jumped into action. He has been my saviour in so many ways, but this will forever go down as the moment I realized I will never take him or his partnership for granted. As our friends called 911, he knew to get her to the front door so she was immediately available for the paramedics and he started CPR.

My husband isn't a crier. In 20 years of life together, I have seen him cry three times. When his grandma died when our son died, and when he thought our daughter was dead. Through his tears and CPR breaths, he kept repeating, "Don't you dare die on me!" I know it was only a matter of minutes, but it felt like a pure lifetime before the paramedics made it. While trying to revive her they asked so many questions, but I didn't process any words until I got in that ambulance. Sadly, we made this exact drive to the children's emergency room 6 times prior - so I knew where we were going but it felt a million times longer in the ambulance.

She spent a week in a coma. That week was pure hell. My husband's last grandparent passed away. Both of our cars were broken into at home. Twice the chaplain was asked to come in and prepare us to say goodbye to her. And there were so many times in that week that I wasn't sure I was going to make it. It literally felt like our world was crashing down on top of us.

I went into pure survival mode to find a way out. Putting blinders on to anything that wasn't in the top priority category for me. I delegated as many decisions as possible. And accepted I only had the strength to be in the present moment, so I didn't care about being in control.

Because I had no control of the outcomes, of my emotions, or what happened next.

When they unhooked our daughter from the machines to see how much of her brain function she lost, they asked me to play music to help her brain recognize familiar sounds. I turned on *Equal* by Odesza. This is our family living room dance song. As soon as that first drum beat comes out of the speaker, we all come running together to dance and twirl to the dance music vibe.

Within seconds that brave girl was bobbing her head and trying to vocalize the words to the song. It would be a few more days before she was able to talk and a few more weeks before she could fully walk again, but she made a remarkable full recovery!

I Lost All Control

We now lovingly call her "Boss Baby" because though she is the baby of the family, at 4 years old she totally runs the show.

While that week of hell appeared to be rock bottom in our lives, it would take changing everything in our lifestyle before I realized it.

After enduring her eighth hospital stay in less than 12 months, her medical care team agreed a change of environment was the greatest chance she had at a healthy life. Shortly after that last discharge, we hastily relocated across the country to escape the setting that repeatedly led to hospitalizations, settling in my grandparents' vacation home.

For several weeks after we moved, I was so lost. I felt like a zombie. I went through the motions, but I wasn't in the present. All I could feel was how angry I was at the situation. How much I just wanted to be in our home, angry at the world for having to leave the place where I finally felt satisfied in life.

I spent 2 months waking up every single day so angry. This was the moment when I hit rock bottom, understanding that I could no longer hide beneath those dark clouds. I needed to discover the tools and resilience to overcome them; otherwise, my life decisions would continue to be the root of my suffering and ongoing depression.

I turned my anger into hustle and decided to work my way out of the situation. Grinding day in and day out to create enough money to afford a new home that was safe for my daughter to live in and a home base for the big kids. Because yet again they were forced to give up their entire life, with no real choice, but to leave everything that was comforting to them.

While the healing journey never really stopped, I had kept it quite surface level when it came to money. It was my true limiting belief, and it was the direct cause of not showing up authentically with my husband and my kids. Having a family is not cheap, and every time I felt fearful about money I lashed out. They love and support me more than I could ever dream, even in my moments when I am not really loveable, and in return, I give them my anger when things don't go as planned.

I flew back to our old town to spend a week with one of my business mentors. I had to get out of the environment that was clouding my emotions to get clear on how to get over my limiting beliefs. Her house feels like home. I was in a good place that week and had a mastermind call scheduled with my Human Design coach.

Human Design is a blueprint of your energy and personality. The goal is to understand yourself better and live in a way that feels more natural and fulfilling. As a Reflector, one of the energy types, I am highly adaptable and sensitive to my environment. I am drawn to seeking clarity and wisdom through observation and interaction.

Sitting in the guest bedroom of my mentor's house, I logged on the video call with excitement!

Immediately, I was asked, "Gabby, how are you doing today?" Before my brain could even process the words, my mouth started moving and said, "I am so scared. I am in a really rough place financially. I feel trapped. And I am worried for my kids. I don't even know where to start, and I feel like I am losing myself." Those ladies wrapped their virtual arms around me and got to work bringing all of their magic.

They gave me whatever permission I was holding myself back from to get help. And while I cried hysterically for an hour, I finally admitted I was scared of money and faced it head on in front of my entire mastermind group.

The Control Was Never Mine to Hold

This time I stopped avoiding my issues. I looked them in the face. I let go of all of the excuses. I took the lessons from forcibly learning to pivot, grow, evolve, adapt, expect the unexpected... and fully started co-creating with the universe.

After diving into the depths of my pain, I got clear on what my happiness looked like. I used my vulnerable self-discovery journey to admit to myself that I don't actually enjoy being in hustle mode all the time. It was a long journey and filled with so many tears.

And on the other side of the tears, I found me. I found a business pivot that allows me to support women by designing a life they love. I found my voice to help others be fully present in their lives without waiting for a tragedy to wake them up. It is the most beautiful ending to a journey that took my joy and my desire to live for most of my life.

As of writing this chapter, we are in the process of moving to Arizona. The place that was recommended as the healthiest place for my daughter to grow up in for her health needs. Through a series of moments where it felt like the stars perfectly aligned, we were landing in the place that was exactly where we were supposed to be.

I am really thankful for the journey that forced me to discover a much slower pace. It allowed us to finally create a family relationship and dynamic that truly makes me say, "I love our life" every single day, even when we are not exactly where we want to be. I wake up every morning thrilled to open my laptop because I am doing work that sets my soul on fire and changes lives every single day. I am enjoying every bit of this journey.

I am emotionally aware enough to call myself out when I do not show up with those around me the way I intend to. I am not afraid to say sorry, and I am not afraid to correct my wrongs. Most importantly I am not afraid to ask for help when I need it. And while the scars remain, they are a testament to my strength, my ability to rise from the ashes and create a life that is not just intentional, but also authentically mine.

So while society has been on this, women should "Stop saying sorry" movement, I am breaking that rule - naturally. Because that is what intentional living is all about, living according to your own values and beliefs.

I'm sorry.

I'm sorry for refusing to deal with my fears. I'm sorry for the chaos I created in my life by turning to avoidance over healing. I'm sorry for waiting so long to step into my full, intentional self.

But I am here now! Fully stepping into myself. Unapologetically removing anything that doesn't support the life I dream of and desire. And I am teaching others to do the same. For that, I am so thankful for the journey that got me here. Healing is not a linear journey. There will be setbacks and unexpected storms. Facing them with courage, vulnerability, and a commitment to self-compassion allows you to break free from the dark clouds of avoidance.

Gabs Hayes

Gabs Hayes is a Mindset & Lifestyle Strategist, Author, and Speaker. She's the founder of the Balance is Bullsh!t movement, empowering women globally to ditch the overwhelm of life's messy seasons and create space for what truly matters. She's also the co-founder of The Brave Start, an all-in-one system for Product Development professionals to launch thriving coaching and consulting businesses.

Gabs was once a corporate climber held back from her dreams by fear of failure and the need to please others. Despite the success and a beautiful family, she felt invisible, constantly on the go yet never truly present. Overwhelm and self-doubt kept her stuck. Through deep exploration of mindset and healthy boundaries, Gabs silenced her inner critic, conquered her fears, and stepped into her power.

Now, Gabs empowers women through engaging podcast episodes, personalized 1:1 strategy sessions and dynamic workshop facilitation. She equips women with powerful strategies to tackle the "not enough" feeling, replace self-doubt with unwavering confidence, and craft a life full of intention and fulfilment. Beyond her career endeavours, Gabs cherishes time spent travelling with her kids, getting lost in books, and revitalizing her spirit at music festivals.

https://gabshayes.com/

9

THE SIXTEEN-YEAR-OLD GIRL INSIDE ME...

EMILY SANDERS

"When we are born, we are born in innocence. When we step into this world, we know only love. So, when we hate it doesn't come naturally, we've got to unlearn it before it's too late. If we only believe...Every race and color, all religions, every creed, we could come together—stop the world for just one night of peace..." ~New Kids on the Block

The Law of Attraction proposes that by envisioning your goals and actively working toward them, you can manifest them into reality. Imagine if everyone collectively visualized just **ONE NIGHT OF PEACE**. Our environment shapes us and, regrettably, there exists a considerable amount of "learned" ugliness that compromises the inherent innocence we are born with.

Growing up in Colorado, I lived in a middle-class diverse neighborhood in Thornton, 20 minutes north of Denver. Raised by parents who instilled liberal values, overall trusting the good in people, I stood out as the sole, fair-skinned white girl on my block, where some of my closest friends were Hispanic and Black. It wasn't until later in life that I truly grasped the significance of those friendships and what the rest of the world's viewpoints were on race. I just saw them as my friends.

I was a true 80s girl who styled her hair with the highest level of teasing, always having *AQUANET* close by. I loved all of the John Hughes movies, bought every new monthly teen magazine, and was obsessed with the New Kids on the Block. Yes, my bedroom was plastered with Jordan, Donnie, Joe, Jon and Danny, from top to bottom.

A dancer, I competed in local and national competitions with my dance studio and had big dreams to someday open my own dance studio – you know, right after I spent a great deal of time as a back-up dancer for Janet Jackson of course. Although, my biggest dream of all was to be a professional model just as stunning and accomplished as the world-renowned supermodel Kathy Ireland.

What Happened to Me

It was fall, 1991, and I was starting my junior year in high school. I received an invitation to visit my friend, Robin, at her college to watch her perform with her dance team at a football game. Initially, my parents were less than enthusiastic. It required weeks of persuasion and showcasing a level of maturity that assured them of my trustworthiness. I even presented the argument that this experience would dispel any reservations I had about attending college. Eventually, they agreed to let me go. I jumped in my cute black VW Convertible Bug and headed to Greeley, home of the University of Northern Colorado.

Upon arriving at Robin's house, I observed her with her friends and the sisterhood they shared. Any lingering uncertainty about attending college evaporated. It was a resounding "yes" in my mind. As we prepared to head to the game, their collective care for me, the non-college attendee, was evident. I made a conscious decision to "turn up the volume" on my maturity, aiming to better blend in with the college crowd. The game was electric, and the sea of cute college guys surrounded me in every direction.

Following the game, we returned to the house to "pregame" for a party. The girls' boyfriends arrived to take us, carrying bags of alcohol with them. While I had drank a bit in the past and wasn't particularly fond of it, my newfound determination to blend into college life led me to believe I should at least grab one drink and hold onto it for the rest of the night. After all, who would know it was my first one, right?

One of the guys handed me a drink called Purple Passion, assuring me it had hardly any alcohol. As a side note-and to clarify his extensive knowledge of this drink - Everclear Purple Passion Liquor was bottled at 26 proof which is 13% ABV (alcohol by volume). Therefore, as a girl at 110 lbs, my blood alcohol would have registered way past the legal limit after having just one and a half to two 12 oz bottles.

I took a sip, and it tasted just like grape Kool-Aid, I could enjoy it without any worries. It went down so easily, I felt relieved that I didn't have to force down beer and pretend to like it. I finished three bottles and grabbed the fourth from the box before piling into the car with the others to head to the party.

If you're a Colorado native, you're probably familiar with the ongoing joke about the unpleasant smell in the city of Greeley (sorry Greeley, but you know it's true). The meat-packing industry's pervasive odor enveloping the city. To add insult to injury, as we entered the house, the scent of marijuana hit me. It was not a smell I was accustomed to. Combined with my impending drunkenness, it was overwhelming and left an unforgettable impression.

It was like a party scene in movies like *Pretty in Pink* and *Sixteen Candles*. Up until this point, my experiences were limited to hanging out with friends at someone's house, watching movies, eating pizza, and sharing secrets. This situation was undeniably intimidating. I was completely out of my league. We committed to a corner of the room, and I was a bit lightheaded, developing a contact high from the marijuana and the fact that I was now drinking a fourth bottle of Purple Passion.

I vividly recall making valiant attempts to conceal the fact that I was merely sixteen years old. As time passed, my tribe gradually drifted away, engaging with others they found throughout the house. Initially, they would come back periodically to check on me, but the time between these visits grew increasingly sparse.

Earlier, I mentioned *Sixteen Candles*...My friends and I all shared the sentiments of LOVE that Samantha Baker, (Molly Ringwald), felt about her love interest Jake Ryan, (Michael Schoeffling). So, you can imagine my surprise and shyness when a guy approached me, bearing a striking resemblance to Jake.

Holding a can of Pepsi, instead of the red Solo cup of beer that others had, he said to me, "Hi, I'm Jeff. How are you, beautiful, what's your name?" I think I may have looked behind me to see if he was talking to someone else. How could it be possible that this gorgeous, older guy was calling me beautiful and wanting to talk to me?

I replied, "I'm good, my name is Emily", distinctly remembering that I was praying that he wouldn't think I was sixteen. However, as we engaged in surface-level conversations, I'm quite sure I made it clear that I was not in college, as I had no idea how to answer most questions. This fact became evident when he went to grab a can of Pepsi and, as he handed it to me, said, "Here, I think you need this to drink for the rest of the night."

"What a sweet guy," I thought, as I clicked the tab and took a sip. As we continued to talk, I lost track of my friends in the crowd. He noticed that I was scanning the room and offered to help me find them. Taking my hand, he said, "Come on, beautiful, let's go find your friends." He grabbed my hand, interlocking our fingers. I felt like the luckiest girl in the room. This gorgeous guy was doting on me, and I was on cloud nine, loving every minute of it.

As he led me up the stairs, the music from the stereo grew louder as we weaved in and out of people's conversations, into a bedroom at the end of the long hallway. There were a few girls sitting on the bed. A light was coming in from outside the window, and he pointed to it saying, "Go to the window and look to see if your friends are outside. I'll turn off the light so you can see better."

As I walked over to the window to find people in the backyard, I heard him messing with the light switch. At the same time, the girls left the room, and I heard the sound of the lock on the door turning. The light switch didn't work, so he unplugged the lamp, turning the room dark. Suddenly, we were locked in the room together alone.

He walked over and was significantly taller than I. Standing behind me, he placed his hands on my waist. Bending down, he hovered over me, his breath heavy. He moved my hair back to expose my neck and began kissing my ear, then his lips trailed down my neck. Despite having had boyfriends and being accustomed to making out with them, I felt very inexperienced. He was quite aggressive, and I was grappling with haziness from all the alcohol and a contact high from smoke. I think I had grand illusions that he would fall in love with me, as if we were in a rom-com movie. I would be his girlfriend and I could come to Greeley every weekend to see him from this moment forward. I was enjoying the attention and felt lucky that he chose me.

He turned me around and started to kiss me. To my surprise, he already had his jeans off and was standing in his underwear. He put my hands around his waist and continued to forcefully kiss me. I was having difficulties "keeping up". At the same time, his hands started wandering further down my body. Before I knew it, he had unbuttoned my jeans and pulled them down around my ankles. Startled, I resisted and tried to bend down to pull them back up, but he prevented me from doing that as he grabbed and picked me up at the waist and threw me on the bed. Trying to keep my composure, I told him I didn't want to do anything else, I wanted to go find my friends. He laughed and replied, "not until we get to know each other more," as he took his underwear off, then pulled my panties down with force.

All that went through my mind was a Sex Ed class that I went to in Junior High, wherein the gym teacher wrote two words on a chalkboard: DON'T & STOP. The conversation revolved around this idea that you should just say NO because saying Don't and Stop together would be confusing. So, I know in my heart that even through the fogginess of how I was feeling I did say NO several times. But it didn't matter, he was too strong and the music, laughter, and conversation that flooded the house outside that locked door drowned out any screams of NO coming from inside that room.

A virgin, I was terrified as he forced his way through me. He took a pillow and pressed it hard over my mouth to stop me from screaming, making it impossible to take a deep breath. He took my shirt, pulled it up, and ripped my bra. Both of my hands worked their way up to the pillow attempting to push it off so I could breathe. The more I screamed, the harder he pushed both the pillow and his force into me. I was scared that he would inadvertently kill me as my neck was strained. He'd either suffocate me or break it. His force got more difficult to resist, so I stopped screaming hoping he would release the force from the pillow. Realizing he was not stopping until he finished what he set out to do, I tried to relax hoping it would be over soon.

Although it lasted only minutes, it felt like hours. He finally pulled away and I was left sobbing and felt the aftermath of fluids from both of us between my legs. He laughed at me laying there shaking asking me, "What are you, fifteen or sixteen years old?" I didn't answer. He laughed again saying that he knew that I was a young virgin because of my small boobs, and all the pimples on my face. Making fun of me for wearing a bra for "no reason", he bent down and picked up a shirt from the floor and threw it on me. "Clean yourself off, you're all bloody," he said as he put his jeans on. By this time, there were people outside the door knocking profusely, trying to have it opened.

He bent over me again to give me my jeans and said, "Not a word to anyone about this. You stay in here for fifteen minutes before you come out, you got it?" I nodded in agreement as he pushed off me and got off the bed. I put my jeans on gently because I was in unbelievable pain. He plugged in the lamp, opened the door, and as he walked out, told those outside that I was sick and needed to lay down, locking the knob behind him.

As I attempted to "pull myself together" I shook uncontrollably with tears running down my face. My entire body felt detached from my head. I felt numb and was most likely experiencing shock. It was a girl's room that I was standing in, and she had some makeup on her dresser. I wiped my face and put some makeup on to do the best to make it appear that I wasn't crying.

I finally made my way to the door, hoping there would be no trace of him. As I moved through the sea of people in the hallway and down the stairs, they made fun of me for getting sick. I walked over to the corner to find Robin's boyfriend. He was not as hazy and could see that there was clearly something wrong. He leaned over to give me a side-hug and asked if I was OK. I told him that I didn't feel well and would love to go back to the house. He agreed to take me as he was looking for an excuse to grab the girls and bring us all back to the house given the hour.

It took what felt like forever to gather up all of the girls and make it back to the car. Once arriving at the house, I maintained my silence and choked back tears choosing not to discuss the events that transpired. As I have never had a very good poker face, I remember feeling compelled to smile and make it seem like nothing had happened. My emotions ran high, and I wasn't sure how to even communicate what I'd just experienced to anyone. How did this seemingly sweet guy turn so evil with this "learned" ugliness in a matter of minutes.

While everyone drifted off to sleep, I was grappling with nausea, vomiting all night, and dedicating special attention to my body. The extreme pain and newly developed bruises between my legs was unbearable. I was also worried I could now be pregnant or have a disease. By 8 am, I penned a note to Robin, explaining that I was sick from the drinking and was returning home. I drove the hour-long drive back home, practicing that same poker face for when I saw my parents.

Driven by the fear of their reaction and the apprehension that it might limit any future activities and consequently, my freedom, I didn't tell them. Not to mention, they would have been shattered. Struggling with a pervasive sense of self-blame, fueled by both the extent of my alcohol consumption and the initial enjoyment I derived from the attention I got from him, I resolved to keep the incident to myself.

However, when I saw my friend, Pam, a few days later at the skating rink where I worked, I had a sudden meltdown and told her everything. She said to me, "Emily, you were raped." Raped! I don't believe that I ever thought of the term-rape. I had to admit this to myself. I was a rape victim now. My first time ever having sex and having to know it as rape, was devastating. She suggested seeking guidance from a counselor at her church. Despite our Christian values, my family didn't attend church. After considering it for a few days, I decided that consulting a counselor might be beneficial.

The Aftermath

As I shared my experience, the counselor seemed more preoccupied with the fact that I was drinking underage and had entered a room with a stranger. Her reaction intensified my feelings of guilt and validated my thoughts that the situation was my fault. To my surprise, she also inquired about the man's race, specifically asking if he was a Black man. Perplexed by this line of questioning and why she would fixate on his race, I responded, "No, he was a white man, why would that matter anyway?"

She went on to explain how she was naturally envisioning a Black man as she listened to how I conveyed my story. Completely confused by her inability to have empathy for what I had been through, along with her obvious racist sentiments, I shut down even more. This was truly the second form of "learned" ugliness that I witnessed in just a matter of days. Ironically enough, Robin's boyfriend, the only guy who recognized I was in distress, was a Black man. He was my true knight in shining armour that night. Reflecting on it now, I regret not having made that connection for her at the time, pondering whether she would have felt guilty for assuming that my attacker was Black. She subsequently offered church-related studies that would "help me" and sent me on my way. Complete waste of time and total disappointment.

In the following months, I found myself retreating to my room, seeking solace in solitude. Despite the demands of my job and my commitment as a dancer/cheerleader, attending practices and games, my thoughts invariably led me back to my bedroom. There, amidst the comforting layers of blankets, surrounded by wall-to-wall pictures of New Kids on the Block, I found the peace I longed for. They became the only five guys in the world I felt I could truly trust; they were a symbol of safety. Even now, as they continue to tour, hearing both their classics and new releases, they transport me back, stirring profound emotions within.

As I attempted to find normalcy in my world, I put a face on and went back to school with my secret. I was enrolled in an off-site elective class, involving trips to a modeling agency in Denver every Thursday evening. It was my favorite part of the week, until now. As I attended this class, the cruel words he used to describe me came rushing back to memory. The derogatory remarks about my small boobs and pimples echoed in my mind, highlighting everything I already disliked about myself when I looked in the mirror.

The modeling world demanded beauty and flawlessness, qualities I felt far from possessing. I felt like an imposter, feeling a profound sense of not belonging. At the end of the semester, the prospect of returning was something I dreaded, so I quit and never re-enrolled as planned. As time passed, the frequency of my thoughts about the modeling dream started to diminish.

Three months after the rape, an old boyfriend, who had graduated the year before, returned home from college for Christmas break and reached out. We went to the theater to see the new movie, My Girl, and went to his house afterward. As we reconnected, I found myself contemplating saying YES if things escalated beyond just making out. I hoped that by consenting and having a different experience with someone I cared about, I could overcome the negative memories of my first time. However, what followed felt like an out of body experience, leaving me feeling even emptier than before. I was probably stiff as a board and living in a mindset of "let's just get this over with". From that moment on, I retreated and didn't pursue dating anyone for the next few years. I somehow navigated through my junior and senior years, eventually graduating in 1993.

As I tried to rediscover myself and liberated myself from the burden of dwelling on the rape every day, excitement for my future filled my thoughts. College was off the table at this point, I wasn't interested. But I was on a scholarship at my dance studio, teaching and choreographing pieces for competitions, even performing in shows throughout the Denver area. Taking and teaching lyrical dance classes was extremely beneficial to working through my emotions, I was finally feeling good about my life. Dance would most certainly be my future.

The Triggers

Just when I wasn't thinking about the rape anymore, something happened that rushed the memories back within seconds. I went to a party with some friends and, as we walked up to the door, the scent of marijuana triggered a visceral reaction within me. My stomach churned; an instant headache gripped me. I found myself plunged back into the vivid recollection of that night. Rushing to the bathroom just in time, I spent minutes vomiting, realizing with despair that the memory would never truly release its hold on me.

Fast Forward to 2012, Colorado was the first state to introduce a plan to legalize marijuana, allowing its sale at dispensaries statewide. Despite my aversion to the smell, I voted in favor of the measure, enticed by the promise of increased revenue for schools (which has never happened as promised, due to federal regulations). I was also not naive to the fact that my kids (who were children at that point) would someday want to try it, and I wanted to make sure it was regulated. The initiative passed, leading to a rapid proliferation of dispensaries.

What I didn't realize was that as marijuana became more prevalent in Denver, it would be everywhere you went: sporting events, concerts, even the mall. The scent continues to trigger bad memories. For years when I encountered the smell, panic set in, accompanied by immediate nausea and headaches - a stark reminder of the body's ability to recall trauma. It is still something I deal with to this day. Although I have been able to control the vomiting aspect and I don't necessarily panic anymore, I have to deal with an immediate headache.

Overcoming My Fears

Determined to overcome my fear of intimacy and have a healthy relationship, I bravely ventured into dating, refusing to let it dictate my future. For years, I had a man in my life wherein he helped me to overcome my fear of sex. I managed to distinguish between the physical act of sex and the emotional intimacy involved in an assault. This distinction has enabled me to maintain a healthy perspective on sexuality, allowing me to experience it in a positive and very fulfilling manner.

Even though I made progress, I frequently grappled with a sense of intermittent emptiness and a longing for something I couldn't quite define. It felt like there was a missing piece of the puzzle in my life. Then, one day, Lisa, my boss at the dance studio, sat with me and painted a picture of dancing in Las Vegas. Pursuing a career as a professional dancer was exactly what I needed. The idea of new scenery and people seemed like the missing puzzle piece I had been searching for.

Viva Las Vegas

In October 1995, at the age of twenty, I loaded up my OH-SO-COOL 1993 teal Geo Storm with all of my teenaged belongings that I deemed essential for years and made the move to Las Vegas. While auditioning for shows, I took on what I thought would be a temporary role as a Customer Service Representative at a credit card call center to make ends meet.

Surprisingly, I discovered I enjoyed working in the corporate environment and aspired to advance up into higher-level management positions. I even went as far as becoming a student at the University of Nevada Las Vegas College of Business. Who would have thought college was going to be part of my future? Not me... Throughout the decade, I was immensely proud of the professional woman I was evolving into and loved the life that I had created. I had the pleasure of dancing professionally while simultaneously advancing up the corporate ladder.

So, there I was, earning a substantial income from both jobs I loved yet, deep down, I still felt a profound emptiness, yearning for that missing puzzle piece. After nearly ten years, in 2004, feeling homesick and sensing the conclusion of my time in Las Vegas, I made the decision to sell my house. This time, I loaded up a full-sized moving truck and made my way back to Colorado. Was that missing piece of the puzzle waiting for me back home?

In the years that followed, I was very driven to find the missing piece that would finally make me whole. I had two beautiful children, and eventually married their dad. I completed my studies at a massage therapy school and started my own medically inclined massage practice. Although I thought my husband was an amazing dad to my children, I later went through a divorce and have been a single mom since 2014.

Throughout this time, I developed a business plan for a spa that included a childcare option wherein parents could leave their children while they indulged in services. I had a strong feeling this business was the missing puzzle piece. I was approved for a business loan in February 2020 and was excitedly searching out office spaces to start the "missing puzzle piece" business!

Finding The Missing Piece

Everyone recalls their whereabouts in 2020, when the world abruptly came to a halt. The announcement of a virus with unknown complications was a lot for everyone to process. Social distancing from loved ones, had a significant impact on our mental well-being. Sheltering in place with my son and daughter, I was suddenly a schoolteacher, and not a good one I am afraid. God bless our teachers!

When the mask mandate was enforced in April, I crafted a homemade mask using a bandana. Stepping into the grocery store, I secured it over my nose and mouth by tying it tightly behind my head. Observing other shoppers with their homemade masks and cautious expressions, as we all maintained a six-foot distance, I began to feel queasy and struggled to breathe.

The more I attempted, the more difficult it became. A wave of faintness washed over me as I found myself revisiting the memory of being suffocated with that pillow thirty years ago. Watching this memory play out vividly in my mind like a scene from a movie, I instinctively reached for the shelf holding hundreds of avocados in the produce section to steady myself, avocados falling everywhere.

After removing the bandana and taking a deep breath, tears streamed down my face, although I wasn't actively crying, a woman approached me, breaking the social distancing rule, to offer help. She inquired about my well-being, but I couldn't recall my response; it felt like she was speaking to me through a fog, and her words didn't register. After a few minutes, I regained my composure, and she helped me to my car. I drove home feeling stunned, confused, and on the brink of a meltdown as I sat down on the couch. Clearly what I'd just experienced was an overdue emotional release about the repressed memory I never spoke about or let myself remember, being smothered by the pillow.

As I sat there, I thought of the #MeToo movement in 2017. For me, it was a catalyst for countless survivors to reclaim their voices. Yet, it was the televised confirmation hearings for Brett Kavanaugh in 2018 that served as an unexpected trigger, resurrecting memories I had fought hard to suppress. As Dr. Christine Blasey Ford courageously shared her own experience during those hearings, I found myself inextricably bound to her narrative. The similarities between our stories echoed through my mind, breaking the dam that held back the memories. I resonated with everything she said, especially when she couldn't remember the house she was in at the time.

The aftermath of political figures that dismissed her experience because she couldn't remember her location infuriated me. If you had offered me a million dollars to lead you to the house that I was raped, I couldn't do it. I have no idea where I was. In the years that followed, I became resilient enough to share my experience with friends and family. That's why the incident at the grocery store was perplexing; I truly believed I had dealt with those challenges.

Getting back to 2020...I called a friend, a trauma counselor I knew would give me much better advice than the woman I met with at sixteen years old. Her advice was that I needed to face my past, acknowledging every nuance of the details. I was to create a timeline of events as part of Free Association Writing Therapy-a raw, unfiltered exploration that would unearth emotions and illuminate corners of my psyche obscured by time and avoidance. She said that as I continue to write, I will activate the memories that are hindering my ability to move forward.

Faced with the keyboard, gazing at the blinking cursor on my screen, it took days for me to delve into the details of that night. However, once I got started, I was in a productive flow, typing away, when my fifth-grade daughter approached me with a math problem. While going through her homework, I kept typing. After a few minutes, she asked, "Do you even know what you're typing, Mom?" To which I confidently replied, "Yes, I do-I am multitasking!" I saved the document and took a break until that evening. When I revisited the document, I gasped as I read the paragraph I had written while assisting my daughter. It was completely different from what I had intended to write.

> "UP UNTIL THAT POINT I WANTED TO BE A MODEL, JUST LIKE KATHY IRELAND. BUT HE HAD MADE ME FEEL SO UGLY AND WORTHLESS, I FELT THAT I HAD NO BUSINESS PURSUING THIS DREAM WHEN I WASN'T GOOD ENOUGH, SO I QUIT MY MODELING CLASSES AND NEVER WENT BACK."

Gazing at my screen, repeatedly reading this statement triggered a profound sense of relief within me. The exercise truly worked its magic. While engrossed in my daughter's homework, my mind wandered and began unveiling the hidden truths buried deep within my subconscious. The revelation that I wanted to be a model was the crucial missing puzzle piece I had been searching for my whole life. Amidst a pandemic filled with fear and uncertainty dominating the news, I was struck by this epiphany. Despite pursuing other dreams and career aspirations, nothing felt as fulfilling as this realization was truly remarkable, my missing piece of the puzzle...

Reflecting on my childhood dreams, I showed my daughter a picture of Kathy Ireland and confessed I wanted to be her when I grew up. She sighed and said, "Oh, mom, that ship has sailed." Ah, the playful banter between a mother and daughter-she's quite the character. I playfully retorted, "No, that ship has not sailed because I never even launched it!" And from that moment, the wheels in my mind began to turn.

I took deliberate steps towards finding ways to heal the sixteen-year-old inside me and restore what had been taken away from her years ago. My private practice massage therapy business has sponsored the Mrs. Colorado® pageant since 2014. In 2019, they introduced a new division that allowed single, widowed, and divorced women to compete for the

MISS title. Having a familiarity with the previous titleholders, the modeling opportunities, and the impactful use of the title to draw attention to their chosen platforms, I considered trying my luck in competing, my platform being Rape Prevention Education. To my surprise and utter satisfaction, I competed and won the title of Miss Colorado for America Strong 2021 on my first try, ultimately changing my life in the most amazing ways.

Not only did it inspire me to become a business coach, but it also led me to collaborate with a local charity called The Blue Bench. Together, we advocate for the implementation of rape prevention education to be on the curriculum in schools. It took me thirty years to realize my soul's true purpose is to share my story. This type of curriculum is imperative as it stands in stark contrast to the limited sex education classes wherein they do not learn how to protect themselves in such critical moments. I also have future plans to meet with State House of Representatives to pass a bill that would require courses such as Safe Dating, Confidence in Dating and Rape Prevention Education courses in our middle and high schools across the state, subsequently introducing it to other states as well.

I aim to challenge the paradigm surrounding the discussion of sexual assault. People toss around the word rape as if it's just an unfortunate event, expecting survivors to simply accept whatever consequences come with it. It's crucial to recognize that rape is a deeply personal experience, and each copes with it in their own way. We must acknowledge each survivor's journey and BELIEVE them, no matter the timeframe which it is shared. It is not a weapon to be used for political gain.

As far as that modeling puzzle piece, as the reigning queen, I had the privilege to explore the world of modeling on different levels. I even found myself emulating my all-time favorite, Kathy Ireland, during a swimsuit photo shoot! As she is an extraordinary entrepreneur, I realized I had been unknowingly following in her footsteps for years.

In matters of love, it took me years to realize the importance of loving ourselves and recognizing our own worth before we can attract the right relationship. No matter the hurt we've experienced, until we can open our hearts fully, free from fear of vulnerability, we won't find the fulfilling connection we seek. There's a quote I often chuckle at, one that questions why anyone would want to fall in love when it can bring so much pain. Yet, I believe love is worth the risk, and I'm determined not to let past pain dictate the course of my romantic journey.

I will continue to wish for the world to embrace ONE NIGHT OF PEACE! And it's essential to remember no matter where you are in life... That ship has not yet sailed, especially when you haven't even launched it...Go launch your ship!

Emily Sanders

Emily Sanders is the Queen of the Bounce-Back, continually reinventing herself. She embodies the spirit of resilience and ambition, a testament to the transformative power of following one's passions and dreams. As a child, she was fueled by her desire to someday work as a professional dancer. So she immersed herself in the world of competitive dance, and choreography. Later she found herself at the age of 21, in Sin City, becoming an iconic Vegas Showgirl. Now at 49 she is a mother of two wonderful children, embracing roles as a dance mom and a lacrosse mom, and finds fulfillment working in business development and coaching entrepreneurial minded practitioners in the wellness sector.

She views her forties as a decade of rediscovery, marked by more lows than highs in the direction of her life. However, she wholeheartedly admits that those challenging periods taught her resilience, which continues to shine through today. During the pandemic, she made extraordinary realizations that illuminated her true path, leading her to discover her soul's true purpose. Her favorite accomplishment, one she never thought she would achieve, came when she let go of her inhibitions and competed in her first-ever pageant at the age of 46. To her surprise and ultimate delight, she won the title of Miss Colorado for America 2021.

After writing an article about Imposter Syndrome for Women Thrive Magazine in December 2023, she discovered a newfound passion for writing. She plans to continue expanding her portfolio, contributing to both books and magazines, as she embraces this exciting new chapter in her journey. She's forever grateful for this experience and knows that it is just the tip of the iceberg.

https://emilysanderslmt.com

10

MANY TRAUMAS, UNBELIEVABLE TRIUMPH
MY JAGGED PATH TO SELF-BELIEF

SHAMERIA ANN DAVIS

Assaulted.
It's hard to believe.
It's hard to accept.
Easy to deceive.

I deceived myself
of a traumatic memory.
How did it happen?
Buried unintentionally?

Or was this suppression on purpose?
My mind protecting me from myself
Buried for fifteen whole years.
My heart and mind begging for help!

Excerpt from *Divinity in Our Lives*, Shameria Ann Davis (2024)

High School

My freshman year of high school, at the age of 14, I fell for a boy who was sweet, doting and genuinely affectionate. He was my first boyfriend. The only problem I saw, really, was that he physically harmed other boys who befriended me. He even pouted on the shoulders of other girls, telling them that I mistreated him, though, of course, I didn't. He told me that I looked like a prostitute for wearing short shorts. He even questioned me over and over again when I didn't make him a priority during the school day. I was constantly confused about what I could do to reassure him of my love and couldn't believe he would say these things.

Experiences with him were so weird. He always wanted to be where I was; he would miss the bus after school to hang out with me and my girlfriends. He lived ten minutes from our house and my mother would have to take him home. This went on for the majority of my freshman year. My mother paid close attention. She questioned me about why he was always around and if I wasn't sure I wanted to spend this much time with him. I was required to keep my bedroom door open, and she popped up in my doorway throughout his time in the house. I hadn't shared every detail with her, but I was certainly uncomfortable, trying to appease him and answer his questions so that he would stop pestering me. When he asked questions about what I was wearing, why someone hugged me or my whereabouts with friends, I responded with an answer to disarm him. In my mother's vehicle, one day after school, he sat in the front seat and began his usual questioning, and it shocked my mother to her core! She was listening and suddenly, she stopped the car. She scolded him, saying that he was not the authority of my life, he didn't buy my clothing, and he was to never question me again. Then, she took him home. I was no longer allowed to date him. She saved me from that relationship.

College

I joined the military at 17 years old so that I had an honest chance at paying for college. I was a straight 'A' student, and my mother held my grades to a very high standard. She couldn't afford to send me to college, but she wanted me to be intelligent. I wasn't allowed to make 'B's' on my report card and I was proud of myself for always making 'A's. I was naturally smart and wore my grades as a badge of honor because they were so important to my mother. I have a scrapbook with every report card of mine from 1st grade through high school graduation. I graduated with honors, in the top 12 percent of my class and headed to college as a first-generation college student, 250 miles from home. I was happy to get away because I felt like I wouldn't have a bright future if I stayed close to home. My family is very loving, but weren't career driven like me.

My sophomore year of college, that old high school boyfriend contacted me out of the blue. He wanted to transfer to a neighboring college and asked for my help with his paperwork, so I helped, begrudgingly. Once he moved, we were friends, so it didn't seem too odd to offer me a key to his apartment. Though I thought otherwise, he convinced me that I was the closest person that he could trust to have a key for emergencies in our new city. A few years passed, and I had met his ex-girlfriend, with whom he also remained friends. I knew very little about their relationship, but they seemed good together. Little by little, I noticed him going out of his way to need my help. I couldn't understand why.

The two most significant times happened while I was at work. One evening, he called during a night shift and asked for help with his flat tire. Of course, I declined. Why would I, a young woman, go to help a young man at night with his flat tire? That just didn't make sense. Another occasion, he needed a ride to the grocery store, and I declined again. He was a grown man, and I didn't understand why he would ask for my help when he had friends closer to him. He and I did not hang out in the same circles.

One day after the grocery incident, he admitted to assuming one day I would be in his apartment... "Cooking naked and waiting for him to arrive as a surprise." This comment caught me completely off guard, but I reassured him that we would never be anything except friends. I was baffled by the audacity he had to expect more than this. I had absolutely no intention of being in a relationship with him anymore.

The following Saturday, during tutorials at my university, he popped up in my residence hall. The residence hall lab was secured by a glass door and wall-to-wall glass windows. Banging on the glass door like a deranged person, he disturbed everyone in the room. He insisted that I give him his key back right then since I had, "No intentions of ever using them or being with him in a relationship." I can't explain the level of fear that I felt at that moment. I've seen firsthand what a possessive man is capable of. How did he even know where I was? The look in his eyes and the anger in his voice was unnerving. He was disheveled and hostile, so I gave him his key, then retreated to my dormitory. Thankfully, there was a security desk blocking visitors from entering without being signed in. He paced near the desk as I left.

I called my mother through tears, and she was afraid, too. I was hours from home, and she felt helpless to protect me. So, she did what she could and contacted his family. My mother's love for me showed up as fear on high alert. She urged his father to get involved and get his son away from that university. She also told him that she would rather go to jail in my defense than to let his child harm me. He asked to meet with me, so I drove home the next day. He had no idea that I was attending a neighboring college and was puzzled to realize that's why he transferred...to be near me.

His son began college on a full academic scholarship at a college in another city. As we hashed out the details, none of us - me, my mother, his father - had no idea that his son was reaching out to me or why. To make matters worse, his father was now paying tuition for the new college. After further inquiry about his pursuits, his father reassured me that he would pull him from school and the surrounding city. And he did just that.

This whole experience really made it hard for me to trust a man. I felt like love wasn't safe. After all, it wasn't even safe for my mother or my grandmother. I know now that that's not entirely true, but at nineteen years old, it was my truth!

History Repeats

My maternal grandmother was a God-fearing and traditional woman with seven children. She suffered at the hands of her husband, experiencing intense domestic violence in her marriage. My mom was the eldest child in the home, often leading her five younger brothers and sisters out the window to escape the violence, no matter the weather.

My grandma experienced some hard battles with her husband, and I'll never forget the story about the day her husband put her out of their home, on the porch, barely clothed in winter. My grandmother eventually broke free from the abuse of her husband shortly after my mother became an adult, through a hard-sought divorce. There are countless stories of the abuse she endured, and this made my mom want a different life.

My mom had three sons and a daughter of her own, me. Along her journey, she suffered at the hands of my eldest brothers' father a decade before I was born. She was forced to move with him at the age of 18 since she bore his child, and it took a few years for her to break away from him and the violence. History repeated itself with my mother, so she chose to walk in and out of relationships to avoid long-term abuse. She felt men were controlling and she didn't like being controlled; she believed that's what caused abuse in the first place. What stood firm was her faith in God, so she never settled in relationships that didn't work for her.

She and my father were married for two short years when he pursued drugs. My younger brother and I share him as a father. He was a drug dealer turned drug user and was incarcerated when I was five years old until the age of 17. Around age six, my mom experienced abuse by another domestic partner. No child should have to witness domestic abuse, it was alarming. Thankfully, she decided to leave that relationship around the time I turned 10. She chose to never remarry and found happiness on her own.

I know from personal experience that domestic violence in a home can be devastating for children and can lead to desensitization. Through my mother's experience, and subsequently, my own experience, a child can inadvertently learn to tolerate violence. I thought it was the opposite, because my mother was open with me about her experiences and those of my grandmother. I thought I knew what the signs were at a young age, but it turns out that I didn't - because perhaps I was desensitized...

The Unexpected

Two short years later, during my junior year of college, the military sent me to be deployed with an infantry unit that had never been integrated with women. I was given three weeks' notice before being involuntarily deployed. That was certainly a recipe for disaster, but it was the Army's time to begin lifting the ban on women in combat. The unit I was placed into was a military unit with approximately 172 male soldiers who had never served alongside a female. 15 female soldiers were pulled into this unit from all over Texas. In essence, none of us knew one another at all. In this military unit, there were three platoons and a headquarters platoon. A platoon typically has four squads of five to seven people, a senior platoon Sergeant, and a lieutenant. My commander, platoon's senior sergeant and all of my squad leaders were male, while our lieutenant was the only female officer of the 15 females assigned to this unit. There were only four females in my platoon including me, which was very uncomfortable.

My time here was tough and isolating. I was a driver for the commander, a primary radio operator, a 50-caliber gunner for the top mount of our vehicles, and up for promotion to Sergeant before entering this unit. I felt so much pressure to be present and lead while still trying to adjust to all the unwanted attention and visibility as a female soldier.

One night, after formation, my senior platoon Sergeant asked me to take a walk. It was customary for us to be alone with male soldiers, especially senior leaders. He walked me along a path, and I became uncomfortable and uneasy because we went beyond eye-view, beyond the vicinity of any buildings, people, or lights. I couldn't tell you how long the walk took, nor what was said. I felt the hair on my body stand and a fear so strong that I could feel my heartbeat pounding. I couldn't feel my legs underneath me while walking.

He walked me to a park-like area and asked me to sit and talk, but, in the back of my mind, I knew talking was not what he intended. I couldn't shake the feeling that he was going to harm me. I had my weapon (a rifle) on my arm, with no ammunition. I had no way to protect myself. The scary thing is that he also had his weapon (a pistol) but I'm certain he had ammunition as a senior leader.

This man was in his late thirties and married with children. He proceeded to forcefully kiss me, and in that moment I froze. Here I am, a 21-year-old woman in a military man's world, thousands of miles from home, and in a unit with no one I know or trust. I had only been here for two months. I knew I desperately needed a plan to get away. But how would I do this? How could I keep myself from being completely raped?

I couldn't think of or utter any words other than, "I have to pee." He ignored me, reaching into my uniform, pulling my shirt out of my trousers, touching me inappropriately everywhere it seemed, kissing and sucking on my neck, and trying to force me to lay down. He acted as though we agreed to engage in this way, though I was surprised. I had never given him any indication that I wanted to be involved with him and it was not okay to violate me like this. At some point, my words resonated that I really needed to "pee". So, by some miracle, and after some time, he stopped. I fixed my clothing, gained my bearings, and headed back. He mumbled some things to me, but I can only recall his strong suggestion that I not say anything to anyone as we started passing by others.

As we got closer to the building, I felt a sense of relief and gratitude. I ran inside. I did go to the restroom for appearances, but mostly, I needed to compose myself because I was shaken. Military environments, as an under-ranked person, often require shared living space. My room was occupied by three other women in bunk beds, so I didn't want to go there. I don't know how long I stayed in that restroom. I was embarrassed that I let this happen. I was afraid that if someone saw me with him that they would blame me. I felt dirty and wanted to disappear. I'm not sure what my next day or next couple of weeks looked like. I can't even remember if I cried...I was sick to my stomach knowing I had to continue serving with him every single day for the next year. How? Would he try again?

Reprieve

Months before I was assigned to this unit, I had a ganglion cyst growing on my right wrist. The vast majority of ganglion cysts are benign and require outpatient surgeries. However, my surgery was complicated and required one week of leave and physical therapy. Being in a field environment is dusty and dirty...not great for sutures. The cyst had grown around the tendons in my wrist on my dominant hand. The surgeon was concerned about mobility post-surgery, as was I.

Recovery from surgery was hard and the anesthesia made me sick. After immersing myself in physical therapy for some weeks, I had an option to return to my deployment. However, the strength in my wrist was not where it needed to be. How would I drive a tactical vehicle or fire a 50-caliber weapon?

To make matters worse, my commander and my senior platoon Sergeant were best friends and demanded that I return to my unit. I never told my occupational therapist what happened prior to surgery, but I believe she could see the fear in my eyes upon final evaluation. The time away was peaceful, but I was full of anxiety about going back. She asked me what I wanted since I wasn't 100% recovered. I'm not really even sure they should do that sort of thing. I simply shook my head, followed by a softly spoken "no" and I left that unit. Personally, I had to deliver the news to my commander that I was leaving. He berated me, cursed me out, and called me weak. Why is it that men who don't get their way belittle and verbally accost women? This behavior added insult to injury. I tried hard not to cry, but failed. There were so many mixed emotions about leaving my mission and the other women. I returned home, but I was not the same.

Delay

I never spoke about the incident, nor that unit, and my silence to myself would inevitably bury this traumatic experience for years to come. The 21-year-old me worked to convince me that it "wasn't that bad". God had given provision to escape that situation and I was thankful. I told myself, "Shameria, you weren't penetrated and actually raped." I reminded myself of the countless stories of military women who were in fact, completely raped and devastated. My experience wasn't that bad, was it? Albeit buried, it wreaked havoc on my ability to trust authority figures and men. I questioned most things at that point and risk-taking of any kind was no longer an option. I also told myself I needed to work towards promotion so that I can be an advocate for lower-ranking and female soldiers.

The spirit of comparison is dangerous. Oftentimes, we compare our trauma to other people's trauma, as though there's a scale. I know I deceived myself by doing this and I further harmed myself by hiding my pain. I mean, I really hid my pain.

Before I left for that deployment, I was in a good relationship in college. I attempted to return to that relationship post-deployment. I moved in with my boyfriend while I searched for an apartment. Everything that he did made me feel like he was aggressive, and I feared he would harm me though he had never given me any indication that he would.

I didn't know then, but that was the trauma guiding my thoughts. After all, I hadn't healed, and it had only been a few weeks since the assault.

One day, I decided to move out while he was at work and live with a friend. I ignored his calls for an entire week until my apartment was ready, and I had a safe space to retreat, recover, and explain. I was afraid to have an argument with him for fear that he might overreact or become aggressive. I'd seen too many incidents with my mother trying to leave her boyfriend where violence ensued. I found a way to justify my perception of his aggression. We never successfully resumed our relationship, and he never knew about the assault.

> I've sat and revisited my relationship to men.
> Prompted by my amazing therapist.
> Had I been the cause of my divorce?
> Full of hypervigilance and chronic distrust?
>
> I had to see myself for the experiences
> and for the shield on my heart.
> To release any responsibility I held.
> Self-blaming tearing me apart!
>
> Through this pain and self suffering,
> The tears just wouldn't flow.
> I had no expectations otherwise.
> Teary agitation and control was, "my show."

Excerpt from *Divinity in Our Lives*, Shameria Ann Davis (2024)

About a year later, I met a very gentle soul, and got married. He was different from any man I knew, and we birthed two amazing little boys. During our fourth year of marriage, I went on a training mission that resulted in yet another close call. But it wouldn't register as such because by then, I'd blocked the memory of the assault. I'd never even told my family or my husband about what happened. This time, I was a senior Lieutenant (yes, I earned a promotion).

Trauma Deepens

During this mission, I was working with higher ranking officers. We were all living temporarily out of a hotel. The mission was up in the mountains in California, but there were no available living quarters for officers on that military installation. So, our common working spaces were the dinner tables in our hotel rooms. A higher-ranking officer and I had some work documents to go over. In a military environment, it is not uncommon to drink after hours while doing business. I was sober and of a clear mind, but he wasn't, unbeknownst to me. He came to my room to review the document and at some point, moved in for an unexpected kiss. With his body weight, he ended up on top of me on my bed. I told him no, and that we were both married. He said he didn't care. I felt immediately anxious and frightened. My heart was pounding, and anxiety overcame me.

This man was extremely muscular and fit, and I had known him to be an outgoing and nice leader. I had also known him to be happily married, so I was completely confused. With all my energy, I pushed him off of me and asked him to leave. He did and I quickly slammed my door closed and locked it. I was an emotional wreck, shaking and crying (something I never do). I called my husband to tell him what happened.

He was thousands of miles from me caring for our toddler! I'm not really sure what I expected, but what I received was a series of questions about why he was in my room and what I might have done to give him the impression that it was okay to kiss me, etc. That response was so hurtful, that I hung up. I've asked myself through the years if I may have a boundary issue. Was I too lenient with men? These were the thoughts that resulted from my husband questioning me. Was it my fault that negative experiences kept happening? Was it them? Or was it me? Sleep deprivation took over my life until I went home a few weeks later. We never discussed it again.

Through those remaining years of my marriage, I couldn't find the space to completely trust my husband again. I felt like I always had to take care of myself. I felt like I couldn't rely on him to keep me safe from harm. My independence had grown so much that I no longer felt like I needed or wanted a husband after almost ten years of marriage. Trauma had caused me to lean so much toward post-traumatic stress that I couldn't see how high I had built walls and my attempts to circumvent past hurts from reoccurring were unsuccessful.

Ultimately, I decided I wasn't the cause of my experiences, and that people are going to do what people are going to do. Why would I accept the blame for a man's decision to cause undue harm to me or to assault me? My hypervigilance was subconsciously reinforced to the point of no return.

We will give ourselves a narrative following trauma that blames others, but blaming anyone other than the aggressor is deceptive to ourselves.

My husband's reaction wasn't awesome, but it was human. Took me more than 15 years to come to that conclusion. I've been divorced for eight years this year. But that's not where the story ends.

Can I tell you that through trauma, your greatest strengths can arise? Can I tell you that through trauma, healing can bring you hope?

I believe that a valuable key to pushing through trauma lies within: I recognized in hindsight that self-perception has been my greatest catalyst for achieving my goals, not an obstacle. I've always focused on empowering myself, and knowing with confidence that my dreams will follow suit. I disassociate trauma... I never quit! I know who God called me to be and I follow suit without second guessing myself.

Let me tell you how I know!

I've gained so much courage from the oppression that I've felt as a woman. My trauma response has always been to prove the odds wrong, because God is always providing the strength I need to do so.

Trauma is paralyzing, but your future doesn't have to be:

In the moments I've experienced my greatest traumatic experiences (and believe me, there are far more than I have shared here), I've always had a freeze and fight later response. Initial responses were always de-layed. I was no superhero in those moments. You can't go back and change anything, but you can move forward! Know that your story doesn't need to look like mine.

My jagged steps looked something like this:

1. Shock: "I can't believe this is happening to me."

2. Retreat or withdraw from the aggressor: "How can I make this stop?"

3. Grief: "Why did this happen to me?"

4. Fight back, progress, and be hyper vigilant: "What can I do differ-ently to keep this from happening again?"

5. Advocate as a coping mechanism: "What can I do to keep this from happening to others?"

6. Reinforce the truth: "A man in the military assaulted me, not the military itself."

Trauma changes us, but that change can propel us to greater heights:

Set some tangible goals. To become a commissioned officer in the mili-tary, you must be a college graduate with a bachelor's degree and be selected either from a rigorous selection process or graduate from a special military training school or college. I worked hard to finish school with trauma in tow, beating the odds as a first-generation college grad-uate, and secured a path to be promoted as an officer. Find a goal and push until you get the results you want! Without setting my goals and reaching them, I'm not sure I'd be as confident in myself.

Traumatic memories can last a lifetime, but we can face our adversity with truth:

Who are you? I've always been a firm believer that when things go wrong, trauma happens or a major problem arises; it is with firm con-viction of who we are that gets us through it. I know and understand that there are people who prey on others, but that doesn't mean that they are the majority or that the victim is at fault. It's them, not you! I may have grieved and asked myself why something happened to me, been reminded that it could've been worse, but those were propellers for me. I'm healing and I get to tell my story and help others. Without my story, many may think they are alone, but we're never alone.

Perseverance

Four years after the college incident with my high school boyfriend, and two years after the assault by my senior platoon sergeant, I graduated with double bachelor's degrees in psychology and political science with honors.

One year after graduation, I was successfully commissioned as an officer through a very rigorous process. I went from enlisted at 17 years old to an officer at 24 years old in a total of seven years in service the hard way! I always believed that females were seen as weak and vulnerable, and that pushed me to prove that mentality wrong.

I also understood that being an African American female was twice the uphill battle in a military force, but I successfully made it into the small percentage of female officers. Did you know that females represent a mere 16 percent of Army enlisted forces and only 19 percent of the Army officer corps? Two years after the incident with the higher-ranking male officer, I successfully graduated with my master's in public health with honors. My goal was to make Captain and retire.

I now see that I had developed a pattern of using educational goals to push through pain. Though my mother had high standards, those would serve me later in life. Beyond everything, learning was a bittersweet distraction. I'm here to tell you that I retired honorably as a Captain with over 20 years of service in 2021 and those numbers I stated reflect service statistics at the time of my retirement. I'm proud I stayed the course.

Delayed not Denied

During my retirement year, I requested counseling to address some of the trust issues that I knew I had, but not necessarily why I developed them. In speaking with my psychologist, she was immediately suspicious that I had experienced sexual trauma because of my extreme hypervigilance. When a mate does something I don't like, I tend to cut things off quickly in an effort to not have them repeat that behavior. I either dated men for very short periods of time or not at all.

My psychologist did a screening with a series of questions like:
"Do you put energy into not feeling certain emotions?"

"Do you trust people?"

"Do you spend time thinking about how things won't work out?"

"Are you overly careful about making mistakes?"

"Have you ever been forced or pressured into doing something you weren't comfortable with?"

With this series of questions and many others as I answered, "yes, no, yes, yes and yes" respectively, the original assault memory came flooding back with a vengeance. I was overwhelmed with emotion, and I could not even fully let myself remember.

The remembrance came with time and patience with myself. I had to peel through layers and layers of ways I've protected myself from what happened. The truth is, I pushed through emotions for so many years, that I hadn't shed healthy tears in over a decade. My trauma response was my strength for 15 years and I told myself that crying solves no problem. The art of suppression became my norm, and I didn't shed happy tears either or express positive emotions regularly. It took me another full year to accept what was and that I needed to strip hyper vigilance from my toolbox...because it was more of a false shield of protection.

That was three short years ago and counting. The person that I am today is a completely different person and I'm very grateful.

So, I broke down my layers,
Piece, by piece, by piece...
I gave myself permission for grace.
Being assaulted wasn't done to me by me.

I can own the blessing in remembering.
I can have no regrets.
I can embrace mistakes and blind spots.
Change can happen through any mess.

Clearing the path ahead as my journey.
Experience doesn't have to be healed.
We can never go back and change the pathway.
But we can grow through feeling what we feel.

Feelings make us who we are.
Enhancing our ability to be in touch with self.
Our reactions unknown are symptoms.
So, let your triggers lead you to get help.

Excerpt from *Divinity in Our Lives*, Shameria Ann Davis (2024)

Belief in self and personal strength holds the power to create either barriers or bridges for ourselves. By transforming our mindset and placing faith in the abilities that God plants within us, we can overcome any challenge and turn our aspirations into realities even when they're born from pain. I became an advocate and I fully believe it was birthed through my subconscious need to protect myself.

Recovery & Love

In 2022, I shared my story with my ex-husband and apologized to him. Although we had many differences between us, many of those issues were connected to my trauma response. I recognized that he only ever knew me as deeply as I knew myself. For us to be the best co-parents, I felt that he should be in the know. We're now good friends.

I'm now engaged to an amazing man who is patient with me and knows my story in full. There is something very calm about his love and our life together. There is also the commonality of our shared faith. I decided to share with him many of the traumas I've experienced, and he's eager to learn more about them and grow with me. He truly wants more of my heart and I'm working to give it freely.

I've also poured much of the love, strength, and care I needed for myself into my legacies, my sons. Jasai and Jonah are both the most aware, intelligent, and compassionate 13 and 9-year-old children known to mankind. They are true reminders of the best parts of me.

I hope this story helps any woman who has been through the trauma of domestic violence or military sexual trauma. May it lead you to overcome and persevere...without hyper vigilance...with healthy responses to your triggers.

Shameria Ann Davis

Shameria Ann Davis is the Brand Confidence Coach. As a proud Texan, retired United States Army Captain and certified coach, she's focused on helping entrepreneurs and business owners get clear on their business strategy, branding and their winning business model. She spent 2 decades working with local, state and government agencies administering health/wellness programming and consulting, leading her to create A Davis Consulting, LLC. Shameria holds bachelors degrees in both political science and psychology from the University of Houston and a master's degree in public health (MPH) from American Military University.

As a credit to her knack for consulting, Shameria is a National Certified Public Manager® (CPM) and an elected official for the Copperas Cove Independent School District nearing the end of her 2nd term. As an avid volunteer, she belongs to a few action-oriented community organizations, including the Marvelous Mu Delta Zeta Chapter of Zeta Phi Beta Sorority, Inc., President of the Alpha Beta Chapter of Alpha Delta Omega Military Sorority, Inc., and President of her local parent teacher association.

She takes immense pride in the progress and achievements of everyday people who are searching for just a little bit of help building confidence and building their brand. She believes strongly that manifestation is the first step in achieving any goal we may set for ourselves or our businesses and is highly experienced in supporting her clients in finding the answers they are looking for. Shameria channeled her dedication to empowering individuals to reach their full potential into writing this book and Divinity in Our Lives, a collection of poems that will not only make you ponder but also evoke a whirlwind of emotions, nudging you towards your own journey of self-discovery. She has two amazing sons, is engaged to a wonderful man and knows that her greatest impact would be to leave a legacy for generations to come.

https://www.shameriaann.com/

11

THE ROAD AHEAD OF ME
LOVING MYSELF AND SELF ACCEPTANCE

ANA M. SANTOS

Reflections and Gratitude

When I sit and reflect on what my life has been, it's inevitable to feel a mixture of emotions. Some of my experiences were really hard times to live through, but others were as wonderful as life itself. Now, I realize that *all* of my experiences have made me the woman I am today. I'm thankful to God for the woman I have become. I'm thankful for the life I created for myself, my children and my dogs. I thank God everyday for the opportunity to become a better person each morning.

Growing up in a world that displays strength and vulnerability as measures of success, I find myself centered as I love my strength and I accept my vulnerabilities. I'm not timid nor scared anymore as I know I can accomplish anything I set my mind to. Now through my journey, I understand the scared little girl I was once. I Love her and accept her when she pops up in my head. I feel love and compassion for her. And I don't freeze anymore or want to be invisible. I love myself. I accept myself.

For those who don't know me, my name is Ana Santos, or Ana La Contadora. In English, it means "Ana The Accountant". Funny because when I was working on developing my brand, I noticed that my clients would answer the phone and say: "I'll call you back, I'm in the accountant's office." Thus, what better name than Ana the Accountant?

Crafting my identity- My childhood

I am 58 years old and I'm writing this chapter at a time in my life where I am grateful and joyful about who I've become and everything I've achieved. Overall, it has been a year of appreciation. Appreciation for life. Appreciation for my existence. Appreciation for my family, my kids, my dogs, my friends, truly everything that surrounds me. Appreciation that God has been with me every step of the way. Appreciation for the opportunity to write my own chapter of this book. And, finally, appreciation for you, for reading my story.

I am the oldest of two children from my parents' marriage. They were both from the Dominican Republic and moved to New York a few months before I was born in July 1965. My parents were hard-working people. My dad had a college degree and worked as an accountant. By the time I was five, they decided to move to the beautiful Island of Puerto Rico. Eventually, they got divorced and my mom moved to D.R. and my dad stayed in Puerto Rico. I was Daddy's little girl. I had a great affinity with him, and he always lectured me on the importance of studying and working hard in school. I strived to make him happy by getting good grades to earn his pride. The plan for my brother and me was always to go to college, get a college degree, and land a job that paid well.

As I near my 60th birthday, which marks a very significant age in my life, it represents a stepping stone. I find myself wiser and joyful and closer to retirement, planning the next phase of my life. I've decided to briefly pause and look back to see what my life has been like and where I'm going. Sometimes, in order to move forward, you must take a trip back down memory lane. This writing, reflecting, and healing process has made me realize that I'm strong, and determined and have overcome all the challenges I have faced during my life. Most importantly, as my daughter says: "What Momma wants, Momma gets!".

When I was a little girl, I was the chubbiest and biggest one in the crowd. I was one of the biggest kids in my classroom and, because of that, I was often teased. I never saw myself any different but over time, that ended up creating a massive level of insecurity and low self-esteem that has taken me years to rebuild and repair. I always tried to hide, never wanting to be seen. On top of that, it didn't help that when I was around five years old, I had a teacher who — maybe it was because I giggled, or I didn't follow instructions right away — punished me by hitting my hands with a ruler and sending me to a corner. I felt humiliated every time I was disciplined. I wanted to disappear off the face of the earth. I felt miserable. I wanted to become invisible. As an adult, later in my life, I came to peace with that teacher and forgave her. "'But the impact she had on me cannot be ignored".

When I was six years old, I went on a family vacation to Santiago de los Caballeros in the Dominican Republic, my parents' native country. My uncle took us to his private club that had pools everywhere. The place had a kid's pool. Boy, I was so excited to play in the kid's pool. It was a hot and sunny summer day.

Growing up, we didn't have a pool, nor did we have access to any pools either. If we wanted to cool off, my mother would take us once in a while to the beach. You could not even imagine the level of excitement I had when I finally arrived at the kid's pool. After being there for about 10 minutes, a lifeguard walked up to me and in a very serious voice, said, "Excuse me, Ma'am, this pool is for kids, not adults. You need to leave." What? I couldn't believe he was talking to me. I looked at him in a surprised but respectful way. I was petrified.

"You have to leave," he repeated. The lifeguard proceeded to escort me out of the pool in order to make sure that I left. I was in shock. I started crying. When I went back to my aunt and told them what happened, my family started making jokes and laughing about it. My mother was not there, so I had no one to run to nor defend me from the lifeguard "'Look at what happened to Ana! Blah..blah...blah...the lifeguard thought she was a woman!". I have never forgotten that day's events. For years, they talked and laughed about it. Ever since I can remember, I have experienced being bullied or laughed at because I was chubby and taller. I felt alone, I felt laughed at over something I couldn't control.

Crafting my identity- Highschool Years

During my high school years, I was one of the chubbiest girls in the class. Luckily for me, I felt t more accepted. I was in a place where I was happy, and my appearance was not an issue. I developed a friendlier personality. I wanted everybody to like me so they would not notice my looks. I strategized by making people laugh. I clowned around, trying to show a kind, goofy personality. I was an extra little bit of everything. Extra nice, extra funny, and always joking around. I was funny and my classmates liked me. Still, inside, I had this emptiness and felt a void within me. I never liked myself when I looked in the mirror. I always felt the ugliest in the room. I didn't like my hair, my clothes, or my body. I couldn't stop comparing myself to others. Thank God we wore uniforms all the time since I was in private school. Wearing uniforms made me feel a little better when I compared myself to other girls. I didn't feel as different when everyone looked the same plus the anxiety of what to wear each morning didn't exist.

Surrounded by my friends in school, I felt accepted, and I wasn't bullied by anybody here. Thank goodness that I went to an all-girls Catholic school. It was only towards the last two years that the school started admitting boys. The majority of my classmates were girls, if you wanted to date and have a boyfriend, you had to find one outside of school. The school population consisted of 90% girls and 10% boys. There were very few relationships within the school and being surrounded by girls made me feel at ease.

Outside of school, I felt as though I wasn't attractive enough to get a boy's attention. I don't know why, but during my teenage years, every time I liked a boy, that boy always liked my best friend, my cousin, or anybody else but me. Needless to say, this didn't help my confidence. In fact, it got worse. Can you imagine? I lived thinking that I wasn't attractive, disliking my appearance, my body, my hair. Basically, not accepting myself completely because I was always comparing myself to others. It's called a comparison trap for a reason. Once again, those feelings of being non-existent and invisible flourished again. It was the only way I knew to band-aid the underlying pain. You have to be careful what you wish for because it comes true. I wanted to become invisible, and I was invisible to boys, where energy goes, focus flows. I had all these wrong perceptions of beauty inside my head.

At 17, I decided that I had enough. I was going to shape up. I did a low-carb diet, and I stopped eating junk food and candies which, by the way, were my favorites. I started exercising twice a day and I played volleyball. During that period, I slept a lot because sleeping was the only way that I wouldn't think about or engage with food. I was on a diet, not a lifestyle change, and my relationship with food ultimately didn't change. I was not eating all the junk food I loved but I missed it and I craved it. I lost about 40 pounds, and I was feeling great! I was on top of the world. I went shopping and I was fitting into 'regular-size' clothes, not plus-size clothing. I went down four sizes! I felt heavenly! Still, I wasn't happy restricting myself from eating like I was eating before.

What a contradiction: I loved my looks, but I missed my old eating habits. I always say that I invented protein shakes because that's what I would do. I would drink a papaya shake in the morning as my breakfast. Lunch and dinner were light on carbs and high in protein. Go figure, making my own dietary guidelines with no professional training (I don't recommend this!). Only listening to advice from the people around me, a fad diet in a magazine or advice given on TV. That's not the healthy way to do it. Now, I look back and recognize how desperate I was to be thin. And that it was my way of dealing with the wounds underneath. Please, if you ever want to lose weight seek professional help. Look for a professional nutritionist.

The moment I got comfortable, what happened? I regained 40 pounds...and a little bit more. The difference was that now I knew the magic secret to losing weight! In my head, I thought, "I did it once, I can do it again." Thus, my road to YO-YO dieting officially began. I wasn't in a position to pay a nutritionist, and my father wasn't going to pay it either. I didn't know anything about nutrition and health, so I handled it my own way. I managed to not gain any more weight, but I sure wasn't keeping it off either. I went back to being unhappy with my appearance. Only I knew it. It was my best-kept secret.

Embracing Adulthood

I graduated from high school in Puerto Rico in 1983 and moved to the Dominican Republic to pursue a career in medicine. I wanted to become a doctor only because I was only focusing on the prestigious career that being a doctor offers. In reality, I didn't have a true calling. I was just mesmerized with the idea of being a doctor and wearing that white robe. That feeling only lasted one semester because I chickened out when I saw what it truly entails to become a doctor. I am scared of wounds, I am scared of blood, and I'm even afraid to see dead bodies in a movie. Why then would I want to become a doctor? What was I thinking?

I don't have what it takes to become a doctor but, realistically, what else can I do? My dad was an accountant of trade and numbers came easy to me. I had excelled at math, algebra, and geometry. Everything that had to do with numbers, I was good at. I said to myself, "Well your dad is an accountant, you should become an accountant, too." So, I changed my major to accounting. I was at peace with my decision. I was truthful to myself, and I didn't feel frustrated about it.

In college, I was made fun of and bullied about my appearance once again. There was a group of guys that would hang out in the corner of the street by my mom's house. Every time I passed by, they would laugh at me because I was fat. There I was, with my low self-esteem backpack again. All I was thinking was, ""What can I do to not be picked on by these guys every day? How can I avoid them?"" My solution was to walk the extra mile to avoid passing by that corner. But guess what? There was another group of guys by the bodegas (small grocery stores) on every corner. Those bodegas were meeting points for guys after school. What was I going to do? I said to myself, "You know what, there is no way that I can avoid them, so I am just going to ignore the negative comments." And when I passed by those bodegas, I walked as fast as I could to not hear the unsolicited remarks. In my head, it was only me being bullied but in reality, I wasn't the only one. I was not at peace with myself. I was unhappy. I was insecure and still struggled with my body image.

I did not know what to do with what I was feeling nor how to handle my emotions. I never told anyone how I felt or what was happening. Big mistake! I always tried to be in a room and become small. I would not even say hello to people. I didn't want to be noticed. I wanted to be invisible again. All the negative feelings I thought I had left behind came back to me. I was unhappy! Unhappy because these guys were picking on me and I didn't have the guts to defend myself. "Why do these guys always pick on me? And why was it constant?"; I told myself that being thinner was the only way I was going to be able to gain esteem and stop the bullying.

So, I did what I always did, become invisible. My resolution was to lose weight. I started watching what I ate and working out and I dropped 40 pounds, and I looked great. I started to take care of my appearance so I would feel good about myself. I felt 'hot' for the first time in my life! I was wearing high heels without them bothering me and I felt like a winner! A 10! Confidence returned. I always loved to dance so I went to parties and danced with everybody. For the first time in my life, I was really living. I wasn't fat, I looked pretty, I fitted into spaces, I wasn't being bullied as much. That, alone, made me feel better. I dressed a bit sexier and wore bathing suits without covering myself with a huge T-shirt. Why not? I worked hard to look (and feel) this way!

I fell in love with one of my neighbours who lived on the same street my mom used to live. He was my first boyfriend. We had a two-year relationship and then we decided to get married. Wow! I got married. I have a husband! I was very, very happy. I got pregnant right away and then moved to Puerto Rico, where my son was born. However, I moved to New York when he was two years old.

Inner Darkness and vulnerabilities- my journey

During that time in my life, I felt like a failure because I did not finish my college career. I jumped into marriage and parenthood, leaving my career behind. I felt like I owed it to my dad since I married prematurely, earlier than he would've wanted me to. Some kids don't follow the plans that their parents create for them. I was one of them. I wanted to become a college graduate. I wanted to get a degree. I wanted to make my father proud. I wanted to make him happy. I would feel his disappointment and I felt miserable to have failed him. For him, after I got married and had my kid, nothing I ever did was good enough just because I didn't follow his plan. But in my mind, I wanted to show him that maybe I had still become what he wanted me to become.

I moved to New York with broken English and a big dream. I wanted to go to college, so I submitted the application. But guess what? I had to sit an admissions test that required writing an essay. I needed to pass that test. I took the test three times while I was taking English classes in college. Finally, the third time was the charm and I passed and was admitted into school. Yes! I went to Baruch College, the number one accounting public school in New York City. I was so proud that I was admitted into that college and into their accounting program. The program was so tough that some people ended up quitting and studying something else. I had a teacher on the first day of school saying, "This is the class that sends people into marketing." That class was Intermediate Accounting. I was determined to succeed at becoming an accountant and accepted the challenge.

I've learned that accounting is more than numbers. Accounting is a way of life. Accounting is the spirit of a company. Numbers tell a story; they leave a legacy. Numbers is the language of business. I always encourage business owners to pay attention to their numbers. Bad numbers break your business and your life, hopes and dreams. Money, numbers, accounting are important in any business. WOW. So much to learn, so many life lessons. This was it for me. I dedicated my life to studying because I wanted to be the best.

Because I studied for long hours, I assumed that my husband would support me and understand that I wanted a better future for us. I wanted to become an accountant. I wanted to get a high-paying job in a great corporation. I wanted to make a lot of money and contribute to the household income so we could achieve the American Dream. I chased the idea that every citizen in the United States (including me!) should have an equal opportunity to achieve success and prosperity through hard work, determination, and initiative.

We lived in a rat-infested building in Spanish Harlem, and I longed to get out of there. At that time, that was all we could afford. I wanted to become better, I wanted to provide for us. But in the process of studying long hours, going to school, and taking care of my son, my husband felt neglected. My son was only three years old at the time. Ultimately, our relationship deteriorated, we were hardly communicating, and fighting a lot. My husband decided he had had enough and left the apartment. I was in shock.

This man was meant to be my forever partner, so I thought. This was the man that I adored. The father of my kid, the one that I wanted to live my life with until death do us part. But God had other plans for me. After I gave birth to my son, I ate all kinds of foods at all times, I was drinking birth control pills, and I gained a lot of weight. Here I go again. Full of self-torture. On top of that, I felt guilty because I was studying so much. I put all of my attention into my schooling because I wanted to get a solid GPA (Grade Point Average). I wanted to graduate with honours. I wanted to give that satisfaction to my dad. I was doing twenty thousand things at a time, and not paying attention to my husband. I'd tell myself I deserved everything that was happening to me. Why was I so hard on myself?

So, I started compulsively eating, eating, and eating more. Till one day I got up, looked at myself, and realized I weighed 290 lbs. "Wait, what are you going to do Ana? What are you going to do?" The inner voices fought back and forth in my head. Well, I was going to get my husband back. I was determined. I forced myself to lose weight again so that I could regain my shape and feel pretty. In my mind, I thought that everything was fixable when I was skinny. Everything in my life was fixable by losing weight, loving and accepting myself.

I was never taught about looking inside of my soul and working on my emotions and self-worth rather than my own looks. So, this time around, I didn't lose a pound. I couldn't refrain from pouring my emotions into a piece of cake and delightfully eating it. My husband and I decided to give our marriage a second chance and I became pregnant with our second child. A beautiful baby girl who was nothing short of a blessing in our lives. Still, the marriage was irreparably broken.

The temporary patch I put on things didn't stick and the fact that we had a new baby in the house didn't magically help. The fighting continued. We were not getting along. The love was gone. There was nothing that I could've done to save my marriage. It was not a matter of being fat or skinny. After the second separation, I was devastated. I picked up the pieces in my life that I could control and kept going because I had two children who depended on me.

Milestones- Finding appreciation

I graduated from college in 1992. My dad came to the ceremony and that gave me a little satisfaction. "Dad, look at me, I got my college degree!" Still, the failure of my separation killed all the hopes and aspirations I had to live the American Dream. It killed my happy ending. Deep down, I felt hopeless. I never shared my emotions with my parents. My mom was living in Florida, and she offered to help me move to Miami. She said it was a great place to raise my children, plus the weather was sunny and hot all year long. I didn't want to stay in New York so shortly after I graduated, I packed my bags and moved to sunny Miami to start a brand-new chapter in my life as a single mother. My ex-husband stayed living in New York, where he completely neglected his ongoing obligations as a father. Back then, I always blamed myself for the failure of my marriage. It was very difficult for me to let go and move on. In reality, it takes two to tango. I thank God for all the great friends that supported my spirit during that difficult time. People who have encouraged me and saw my potential, not my looks.

In Florida, I started working as an accountant and moving up the corporate ladder. It wasn't easy being a single mother and working at the same time, but I was determined. In 1998, an opportunity was presented to me, and I decided to get a Master's Degree. I had the support and help of my mother. She helped me tremendously with my kids. It was a year-and-a-half, weekend program that offered great flexibility for working professionals. I jumped on that wagon and started the program. Time flew by and I graduated from Florida International University with a Master's Degree in Taxation in December, 1999.

Mission accomplished DAD! Every accomplishment I had; I couldn't help but think of him. Think of what he would think of me. So now, not only did I have a Bachelor's Degree in Accounting, but I had a Master's Degree in Taxation. At last, Dad was happy. I saw the look in his eyes when I showed him my diploma. After a whole lifetime spent trying to get his approval, he finally showed how happy and proud he was of me. My dad was not a loving and affectionate type of guy. His love language was through actions and acts of service. Now I understand it. I was happy with myself. I felt accomplished and It had nothing to do with my looks. As a matter of fact, I was 300 lbs when I graduated from FIU, but for the first time, I could still access a level of happiness and pride. My looks didn't matter. I completed my Masters Degree!!!!!!!!

Unleashing my own light

I made myself fully believe, when I was younger, that happiness was only obtained by being thinner. When you face low self-esteem associated with bullying and humiliation and you grow up wanting to be invisible, you think you are on top of the world when you are thinner. "Nothing tastes as good as thin feels," That's what they say. Well, here's what I say to that: What about self-love and self-acceptance? Why do I have to be thin to feel good and to feel accepted? Why do I feel like something is wrong with me if I'm not thin? These and more questions came to my mind every time I would confront the chubby girl that lived in my head. I decided to look for answers to all my questions.

When I hit my heaviest weight in 2004 - 311 lbs - I decided to get a gastric bypass. At this point, the gastric bypass was necessary for medical reasons- high blood pressure and prediabetes. There's a process to undergo medical exams and psychological evaluations in order to determine if you are a good candidate for the surgery. In April 2004, I got the gastric bypass surgery, and I lost 100 lbs in less than a year. I decided to work on myself from the inside out too and got nutritional and psychological help. I took the road to self development. I wanted to lift my spirit up. I worked on my self-esteem issues and I'm not that hard on myself anymore. I am kind, compassionate and loving to myself. Enough was Enough. No more comparing myself to others. I forgave everybody who harmed my spirit by bullying me. Most importantly, I forgave *myself* for being so hard on me. I cleaned my soul and rewrote my story.

Let it be said that this girl is not a victim anymore. The chubby girl in my head is happy. I am proud of myself, and my accomplishments and walk with my head high. I accept myself as I am, and I recognize that God made me beautiful. Those negative experiences made me who I am and showed me the path to becoming the best version of myself. I freed myself of the cage that I constructed for myself. I stopped comparing myself to others. The limitations only existed in my head. My body is my temple and I need to take care of it. I want to live longer. I want to work out, not because I have to but because it gives me energy. Zumba for me is the best!!! I love myself, I love my hair, and I learned the power of positive thinking. I love the way I look; the way God made me. God loves me and he created me the way I am. Who am I to question his creation? I look at myself through his eyes. I'm his perfect creation. There's nothing wrong with me. I'm full of life, vibrant and happy. Like Whitney Houston sings, "The greatest love of all lives inside of yourself." When I stand in front of the mirror, I tell myself how beautiful and smart God made me. I feel pretty. I now have the confidence to walk onto a stage and talk to people about the importance of accounting and numbers in their business. I have done a lot of personal development courses and coaching sessions to overcome my insecurities and I recommend the same to anyone who feels like I felt and wants to hide away. Now I am visible and the fact that I'm sharing my story with you all is proof of that.

Ana M. Santos

Ana M. Santos is a money mindset coach, accountant, tax expert, speaker, published author, and successful entrepreneur. She specializes in making the overly complicated simple when it comes to your finances, and she is on a mission to help you take control of your money so you can turn your dreams into reality. Numbers is the language of business. She is here to help you win, NOW! She holds a Bachelors Degree in Accounting from Bernard Baruch College and a Masters Degree in Taxation from Florida International University.

She was born in Brooklyn, NY of Dominican descent and raised in Puerto Rico. She is a mother of 2: Nelson, 37 and Annamarie, 31. They have been her inspiration to succeed in life. She wants them to feel proud of the woman she has become. She loves to be surrounded by friends and family. Her passion is to see the success of her clients. Currently, she finished Theological studies in the Alpha & Omega Bible College in Miami, FL. with a Salutatorian award and is completing Tony Robbins Leadership Academy.

www.anamsantos.com

12

EMBRACING THE HIGHS AND LOWS OF EXISTENCE EVER ENDING A NEW BEGINNING

STACIE A. FORD

Ever thought you had it all, only to watch it disintegrate right before your eyes?

As a forty-something-year-old woman, I'd like to consider myself well-accomplished, confident, and determined. Before 2020, I thought I'd had it all: The family of my dreams, the career, stability, peace of mind. However, in March that year, that 'all' came to a crashing halt. As the world shut down during a global pandemic, I was tossed into a whirlwind of despair, defeat, and grief. Have you ever lost all hope of recovering from life-threatening situations? The fear is all-consuming, paralyzing, and debilitating.

I've come to experience and know these inner monsters up close and personal. I once believed that hard work would grant me a life free of struggles and hardships. While there's some truth in that, life is unpredictable. An elder once told me, "If you want to make God laugh, tell him your plans." So, let me tell you about the time I had to lose it all, only to make one of the biggest comebacks I've ever known. Thankfully, I am grateful for my story now; had I not experienced such loss, I couldn't marvel in the joy of renewing my life, my purpose, and my passion, and become the comeback goddess that I am today.

Determination

I grew up in a suburb minutes outside of Detroit, Michigan, in a two-parent household with one older sibling. For the most part, my childhood was stable and healthy. My parents did a pretty good job of making sure we had a great childhood; however, money was an underlying issue. I saw my mother worry about money, like the times they were late on rent due to a job change, or the times she'd open the mail and see the pink late notice for the water bill. Looking back now, I know that their financial insecurities informed my own money blueprint later on in life.

As a kid, I anxiously watched my parents and their concerns about money. Seeing my mother panic at the sight of a pink late payment notice in the mail, would cause much worry for me as a little girl. I'm sure my parents never wanted me to worry over the concerns of adults. However, I did, I worried a lot about my financial security and my future.

I suppose those early imprints instilled a drive in me to not experience the same concerns my parents had; I knew that a successful career was the answer. I decided I would be one of the first in my family to obtain a college degree. As a Black woman raised in the 80s, going to college was the ultimate measure of success. So, naturally, that became my goal. Making my family proud was a big deal. In my mind, a college degree was the answer.

I attended college after high school with the assistance of grants, loans, and working to put myself through school. It wasn't as easy as I'd hoped; I struggled to do it all, but I didn't want to burden my parents with another bill. I couldn't bear watching my mother worry about how they would manage, so I did what I could on my own. However, sophomore year

I was met with embarrassment when I found out I didn't have enough aid for classes. I was so desperate to finish school and have my dream career that I took a friend up on a bet to work in a nightclub to pay for school. I absolutely HATED it. Still, nothing was going to stop me from finishing my goal of getting that college degree, not even the disrespect I endured from the patrons and workers of that disgusting bar. I was determined to make it no matter what, until...

At the age of 21, I got pregnant. How could I be so careless? What would I do with a baby, how would I finish school? Here I was, a single mom-to-be, struggling to finish school. To add to my worries, after I had my daughter, we were abandoned by her father, a longtime boyfriend, who promised that he'd be a hands-on father. I was heartbroken. And here I was again afraid of letting my parents and now my daughter down. Carrying an immense amount of guilt of becoming a single mother, I stopped attending classes. I fed myself stories of failure and stereotypes about being another Black single mother who would end up on welfare. Still, I had that same, strong determination to prove that theory wrong.

I was going to finish what I'd started, I had to. A year later, I enrolled into college again. Changing my major this time to nursing. My path to becoming a nurse wasn't easy, to say the least. After a few years of evening classes, working crazy hours, and applying to nursing schools in Michigan, I was finally accepted into a nursing program in Ohio, a three hour commute each day. Just as I was admitted into school I was married and had a son. I had more reasons to obtain my goals. I had a family and more responsibility. That's the thing about a woman with a plan, we'll get it done no matter the cost! I took the long trek to Ohio every day for years and finally I became a nurse! During that time, we also purchased a home. I was living the dream until mid-2000 when life threw me one gigantic curveball. Up until then my personal life and career were thriving. I had the respect of my family and peers. I was healthy, and living a flourishing, balanced life. Until I noticed something was off health wise. In the mid 2000s, I began experiencing migraines that only grew worse in time. I became debilitated for days at a time with blurred vision and numbness in my arms and legs. This went on for months without me uttering a word to anyone, mostly because I was afraid that something was seriously wrong.

I know, you're thinking, "Why wouldn't she say anything if she feared the worst?". Well, as a nurse I'm not always the best patient; I tend to self-diagnose and ignore signs out of fear. After all, taking care of others who are ill did cause some paranoia. I ignored my declining health, hoping that it would improve with proper rest, nutrition and exercise. Let's just say, that was the wrong thing to do, it definitely didn't work.

After many months of chronic symptoms, I decided to stop being afraid and find out what was going on. I had worked a 12-hour midnight shift in the ICU with a paralyzing headache that barely let me get through my shift. Being at the hospital already, I begrudgingly went to the ER instead of home. That ride on the elevator was one of the longest in my life. I played out the worst-case scenarios in my head, reviewing all of my signs and symptoms. Was I having a stroke? Tears in my eyes, and full of sheer panic, I entered the ER.

After several hours of labs, CAT scans, blood pressure checks, and MRIs, I was told that everything looked normal, and I was probably overworked. Whew, what a relief, all of those 'what if's' for nothing. I was relieved to hear that stress and dehydration were the culprits. Hearing, "You're discharged to go home," was music to my ears. I took the discharge instructions to follow up with my primary doctor and headed home. Later on, a thorough exam with my doctor was met with more of the same; she diagnosed me with cluster migraines and referred me to a neurologist. I finally felt like I was getting some answers and excited for an easy solution of medication and monitoring.

What I thought would become a simple appointment ended up with me reeling in fear, panic, and terror once again. The doctor checked all of my vitals, my past medical history, and performed a spinal tap. I'd never known a doctor to do so many tests for migraines, so I knew there was more to it. Three days after my MRI, I received a call from the doctor. He confirmed the cluster migraines diagnosis. He then followed up with the words I dreaded. "Multiple sclerosis." I felt the air leave my lungs and pure fear overcame me.

As a registered nurse, I'd taken care of patients with MS. I was familiar with the disease and its effects. MS can cause loss of all bodily functions and death. Reeling from the news, I thought about one of my favorite comedians, Richard Pryor, who suffered from MS and eventually died from it. I was completely blown away. My brain flooded with questions. Was this hereditary? How would this affect me and my family? Would I become debilitated? How would my quality of life be affected? The dread of the circumstances weighed heavily on me. I often wondered if I would end up like so many of the patients I had cared for...if I'd end like one of my young patients with MS who frequented the ICU I worked in.

Her husband would sit with her day and night with terror and pain in his eyes, always searching for a glimmer of good news. I'd sit at her bedside with him, offering support and reassurance. Would that become my very own reality now, too? After the phone call, I had a panic attack that left me gasping for air as I lay on the floor with tears streaming down my face. Two weeks of living in terror awaiting my follow up appointment. Two weeks were spent researching and reading, in anticipation of what my life may look like with MS.

After weeks of mental torture, I had an appointment with my doctor to discuss my case and treatment. He informed me that the form of MS I had was known as 'relapsing and remitting', meaning that I could go months or even years without any issues, or have ongoing consistent symptoms. He believed that I had a chance of staying in remission with my healthy lifestyle and steroid therapy.

Relieved, I immediately started the weekly infusions. I experienced success; the migraines disappeared and the weakness in my hands and legs was gone. However, the side effects were nasty! My appetite was non-existent; everything tasted like metal. Although I am a nurse trained in Western medicine, I have always believed in Eastern medicine and holistic practices.

After consulting with my neurologist and gaining his support, I decided to try Ayurveda and Chinese medicine. I also adopted a meditation practice to alleviate the anxiety and stress. These practices helped me to totally stop taking the medication prescribed by my neurologist. For years I lived a relatively symptom-free life, with an occasional flare-up here and there. In 2019, I was accepted into the Masters Doctorate Program to become a nurse practitioner.

I avidly took care of my mental and physical health, regularly working out and eating healthy. Life was GOOD! That is...until I started experiencing neck and back pain that no amount of rest or medication could alleviate. "Oh gosh here we go, what is it?" I thought as I dreaded going to the doctor. I was afraid of receiving bad news; however, I didn't put it off this time.

A trip to the ER revealed that I had two herniated discs in my neck. Dumbfounded, I couldn't understand how that could happen; no injuries, no accidents, I was at a loss. Nonetheless, here I was with an injury that no-one could explain, including myself. I was assured that a few weeks of physical therapy and anti-inflammatory medications would solve the issue. Sounds great and promising right? Wrong! The pain grew worse.

Taking care of myself became a task; I had to depend on my husband and children for my basic care. Although grateful for the support, I was embarrassed. It was a hard pill to swallow, letting my husband give me a bath and having my daughter wash my hair. Although much appreciated gestures of love, at 39 years old, this wasn't the idea I had for my life. Month and months with no improvement. Physical therapy visits turned into pain management treatments with spinal epidurals and electrical shock pain therapy that didn't work.

During one of our bi-weekly visits with my primary doctor, she shared her concerns about my noticeably declining mental and emotional state. "Honey, I've been reviewing the notes from the other doctors, your psychological report, and your exam results. You're dealing with severe depression; I think we need to start you on some medication". Worried, I asked her, "When do you think I'll go back to work?" I never imagined her response. "Well, it looks like you need surgery for your spine, the treatments haven't worked. I'll refer you to someone."

In 2020, I rang in the New Year with hopes of a fresh start, renewed health, and reclaiming my independence and smile. It had been months, and it was time to take back my life! Six days into the new year, I had spinal fusion surgery. According to the surgeon, everything was a success. I'd heal for five weeks and start therapy by week six. I'd be fully recovered by week eight and back to normal. Dear god! Words I had been waiting to hear forever, "I'd get my life back".

The circumstances not only impacted my health, my finances also took a hit. I wasn't yielding my normal income, leading me to depleting a small nest egg I had saved up. Yes, disability insurance is awesome, but being paid significantly less, I had to make some hard financial decisions. I had to get back to work sooner rather than later. Eight weeks later I was devastated at the decline in my progress after surgery. I was barely able to walk, and I fell at home causing more complications. I took pain pills every few hours, something wasn't right! Following up with my surgeon began to feel pointless as he kept assuring me that the surgery was a success and offering me more pain medication to cope. I didn't want to mask the pain, I wanted answers.

Broken Promises and Lost Dreams: A Chronicle of Despair

Up until now, I had a deep trust in my healthcare team. That was diminished the moment my surgeon made a remark hinting that I may be drug seeking, as I cried about the constant pain I was experiencing. For the first time ever, I knew what it was like to be a Black woman, whose health wasn't being taken seriously.

Tearfully, I left my surgeon's office and never returned. That was a painful awakening that has stayed with me, as I think of how many more are suffering without resources to advocate for themselves. I knew what I was experiencing wasn't normal. I made an appointment for a second opinion with one of the nation's top spinal surgeons. I'd had experience with him years prior; he'd been a suggested surgeon for my father. While he had an immense reputation for being one of the best spinal surgeons, he also had a reputation for lacking empathy with his patients. Making the appointment I thought to myself, "Well, he may be a little crass but at least I'll get real answers."

My appointment with the specialist was very thorough, he took his time reviewing all of my MRI and CT scan images. After minutes of silence, he finally looked up from his computer to address me. In a flat tone, he told me everything looked fine. All my hopes of finally getting some answers for the unsteady gait, intense pain, migraines, dizziness, and numerous falls, and all he could say was, "Everything looks fine, I don't know what else to say?" I was an inconsolable mess. I was fuming inside. Why would no one give me answers? Did I need a psych evaluation? Was all this pain in my head? I was living a nightmare. I sat in his office, a shaking, sobbing, 'ugly crying' kind of mess. I believe that the specialists' heart grew a little that day, as he could sense my desperation for answers. He asked me to sit for a moment while he and his colleagues reviewed the images together. Sitting, waiting, and too afraid to get my hopes up, I sobbed, fearing I'd never live my life as I once lived it. I feared I'd never work again, never enjoy intimacy with my husband again, never live a day without pain pills, heating pads or topical ointments again. Was this my new normal?

After what seemed like hours the doctor and his colleagues returned to the office, they did see something. What had started as two disc herniations ended with two additional herniations and a narrowing of my spinal column, which caused compression on my brain stem. Typically, this could lead to paralysis and/or memory loss, as it was one of the worst cases he had ever seen. He called it Atlanto-axial subluxation. Although the initial surgery was a success, the additional problem areas were not only causing more issues, they were inoperable, being so close to the brain stem. The rarity of this complication was dangerous and could lead to complications in my mobility. He'd only seen rare cases like this in children born with cerebral palsy and other birth defects.

He gave me answers, but no solutions as he stated, "You'll just have to live with it. Surgery could cause death. I wouldn't do this surgery on you; you'd end up paralyzed or dead." Did I hear him properly? As the world had shut down from a global pandemic, my own world was shattered with just a few words. These words didn't sit well with me, they actually assisted in my spiral into darkness, loneliness, and withdrawal from existence. Hearing those words loop through my mind every day diminished me into a shell of my former fun-loving self. Every aspect of my existence was impacted. I wasn't going back to work, my personal life was gone, and looking at my bank accounts just about sent me over the edge.

My husband did all that he could, but I felt guilty putting so much pressure on him. I've always taken pride in being able to hold my own in any situation. Not this time. MS attacks the muscles and the nerves, so it all made sense; the muscles, ligaments, and nerve fibers in my neck atrophied and couldn't support the cervical disc, causing the disc herniations, misaligned vertebrae, and the weight of over ten pounds of skull and brain, crushing the spinal cord.

Life as I had once known it became so unfamiliar. I cried every single day out of frustration, anger, despair, just wanting to be "normal" again. A day without pills, a day of walking without taking breaks, a day to cook a meal without sitting down every five minutes, a day to put a shirt over my head without help, a day to carry my own bags, climb into a car unassisted, or wash my own hair.

I spent so many days helping my patients and their loved ones through some of the hardest times in their lives, yet I had no idea how to help myself. Everyone could see the changes in my personality, even the physical changes to my body were painfully apparent. I lost over 40 pounds. As a once avid gym rat, there was no sign of muscle tone in sight; I was frail and weak. My family felt helpless and concerned.

Unseen Struggles, Unheard Cries

As a mother, the last thing I'd ever want is to see my children suffer, knowing I can't take it away. I imagine that's how my mom felt the day she looked at me with sincere concern stating, "Watching how this has affected you, I've seen the light leave your eyes." Something about this sentiment broke me. But she was right, the light was gone.

As much as I pretended that I was going to be okay, I had lost hope and had thoughts of suicide. I had hit rock bottom, exhausted and yet still holding onto a possibility of good news. In my efforts to get things together for my husband and children, I began looking over my finances. I carefully reviewed my life insurance policy regarding the stipulations of death caused by suicide. I researched how to take my own life without it setting off red flags that would prevent my life insurance policy from being paid.

Accidental overdose? That seemed to be the easiest, as I was on tons of medications. It wouldn't be too far-fetched if I accidentally took too much. As much as I wanted to end the misery, I kept hearing the intuitive voice reminding me that I hadn't come this far without purpose. As each day passed, I'd muster up the courage to make it my last, only to find another reason to give it one more day.

My daughter's graduation. I couldn't miss that huge milestone; she'd worked so hard! My son was still young and would be unable to understand where mom had gone. I couldn't do that to him, he was just a baby. Maybe I'd explain to him in little layers how death works, I thought. My husband raising the kids alone didn't seem fair, that would be selfish of me to leave him with the responsibility, but at least he would have support.

And what about my parents? My father was already battling cancer, it would all just be too much for them to handle. The thoughts bounced around in my head like a ping pong. I'd decided to get things in order and get it over with. I planned to be gone by my next birthday. I refused to be confined to a bed, deteriorating away. I was going to do this on my own terms, I just had to make sure they were all okay before I left.

The rational and wounded parts of me warred day in and day out, negotiating and bargaining. In hindsight, I know my meditation practice kept me going, as it helped me process the rush of emotions with a clearer view. Meditation subtly strengthens our intuition and emotional intelligence. That intelligence and inner voice that told me not to give up is what I now know has kept me going, causing me to really think of my purpose in life. It helped with that inner knowing that told me this was far from over. I didn't know exactly how it would all work out, after all, nothing had worked so far. But I was willing to keep going even when I hung on by a thread.

Dawn of a Fresh Journey

As I hoped and prayed for changes to my physical, mental and emotional health, I had to also come to grips with my financial health. Before going onto disability, I made a great salary by society's standards, but I wasn't great at managing it. My lack of money management skills became painfully evident. I didn't come from a financially-savvy background. My parents and immediate family were working class and did the best they could, however, money management wasn't something we discussed. I could now understand those days of panic and worry I'd watch my mom experience when the pink late notices came in the mail. I was determined to not have my kids know that same feeling I had as a child.

Up until now we were a two-income household. I was determined not to leave yet another burden for my family. I had to clean up this financial mess. For years I felt helpless about my health, so I decided I would do what I could to alleviate the financial burden. Looking over my life insurance policies months prior sparked a curiosity about how they worked, as well as how money worked in general. For the first time in ages, I was excited to learn again, to feel that I could deliver some type of value again. I decided to get my life insurance license and read as many books about finances as possible.

Coincidentally, I had seen a post from a fellow nurse describing her new venture in life insurance. Many nurses were burnt out from the pandemic and looking for an exit strategy. Here I was trying to figure out how to get back to my career in nursing, while many of my colleagues were leaving. I wondered if that was a sign. I had dreamed of owning a business for years. Never in a million years would I have thought I would leave healthcare to start something new, but at this point what choice did I have? To pursue other options, I reached out to that nurse to get my life insurance license.

This new beginning was something I was excited about, which is something I hadn't experienced in years. I could still help others, work from my home, and potentially get out of debt. I became a sponge wanting to know everything about money. I engulfed myself with learning about money psychology, budgets, debt, investing, retirement, credit, studying every day from my bed. I put my stimulus checks to use by becoming licensed in personal finance.

I utilized scholarships to gain access to financial coaching programs. I also learned something even more valuable than understanding how money works: I learned that it's always possible to adjust to life circumstances and use the changes and challenges to rebirth something new if you remain open to new possibilities. I was open to learning something new to leave my family in the best position possible. I also learned that I knew more than I gave myself credit for. I learned that I was good with money, I just didn't understand it and how to properly manage it. I took it upon myself to have fun with learning and putting what I learned into practice in my own life.

I managed to eliminate over 30K in debt, increased my credit score over 150 points, and learned how to manage both my personal and business finances. I had made this into a profitable business. *And* I did all of this on less income than I was making as a RN. Finally, for the first time in my life, I felt financially secure and like a badass with my money!

In my time of loss, grief, and uncertainty, I had found a new passion. I liked the feeling of financial empowerment; I wanted others to experience it as well. What started off as a need for my own life turned into a passion to help others with those same needs. I understood what those worries felt like, I understood the feeling of trying to stretch that last hundred dollars between food and kids' school supplies. I understood the feeling of an overdrawn bank account, hoping to make it with your last few dollars until the next payday. It was a feeling that I hated, one that added an insurmountable amount of stress to my already overly stressed mind, body and spirit. In those relieving moments, I became more inspired with a sense of purpose. I would help others achieve this same sense of relief.

Finding the Will to Prevail

Being more mindful of my thoughts helped me to stop thinking of my diagnosis as definite. I knew that the MS could still go into remission, so I began to eat foods that help with inflammation and gut-brain health. I did chair yoga from home with videos on YouTube. I had found my fight again. My days of laying in bed worried, anxious, and powerless turned into days of hope. I developed an ability to transmute some of my worst days into some of the best days of my life. My newfound excitement created the optimism I needed to get my life completely on track.

I researched my diagnosis daily, looking for answers every night while my family slept. One late night in bed scrolling the internet, I saw a video that sparked my interest regarding the old talk show host, Montell Williams. He also had MS and often talked about his journey on his show. In one of his episodes, he interviewed a spine specialist who had helped him tremendously. I decided to look up the specialist and couldn't believe what I read. Not only did he specialize in my condition exactly, as there are only a few in the country, he was located close by. I was in disbelief! My angels had been listening to my prayers, and the answer was less than 10 minutes away. At 3 a.m. I sat crying tears of joy as I heard the words, "It's your time, this is what you've been asking for." My intuition led me here. I was elated with excitement!

I called to make an appointment. He was booked for a month, I told them I was willing to wait! Imagine my surprise when I was informed that one of his former colleagues, who also specialized in these special cases, was accepting new patients. I called and made an appointment with her. She was nearly two hours away, but I was willing to make the trip. Everything seemed to be falling into place. That following week, I met the doctor who not only changed my life but who helped me rebirth a new one. She not only answered all of my questions, but she gave me hope. She assured me she could get me back on track. She specialized in holistic medicine and spinal correction. The perfect combo!

That day, I was given back everything that had been taken from me: peace of mind, stability, hope, dreams, my smile, my drive, my motivation, my life. I realized I was getting a fresh start in every way. As the months went by I saw glimpses of my old self returning. My light was back!

So much had changed. I'd helped myself along with numerous individuals in a way that I loved and truly became financially confident. My passion to help others have a healthy existence was still there, I had found a new life-giving way to aid them. The loss, and devastation I'd experienced for over three years morphed me into a new person. I transformed into a more determined, courageous, mindful, and compassionate warrior. I touched the hem of defeat and refused to give up or give in.

Trust me, I was shocked that my circumstances birthed a new mission and career. It was a drastic change, however it manifested out of necessity and fate. From the lows of adversity emerged a lotus, a beacon of rebirth, strength, and resilience. Divine Wealth Solutions was born with a vision to economically empower women entrepreneurs.

The mission of my business finance solutions agency is to empower more women business owners to close the gender gaps in entrepreneurship, to ensure that each woman has access to financial education, resources and opportunities to succeed and thrive abundantly in both their personal and business finances.

Through my own need to reinvent myself, my finances and my career I discovered that not only are women the fastest-growing group of business owners, but they are also the most disenfranchised economically. I believe that women who are in positions of power and in control of their own finances not only have a great impact on their families and their legacy, they are in positions to make a great impact in the community. This mission is not only necessary; it's personal. My journey of self-discovery and resilience helped me to gain a new respect and excitement of embracing change fearlessly.

To you, reader, I wish to say: Better times are ahead. Always. I learned that through my resilience, nothing can keep me down, positive thoughts are imperative in this life. I am grateful I didn't give up; I am grateful that I fought for my life, even when the experts said there was nothing more they could do. There was an inner knowing that this wasn't the end of my story, it was only the beginning. The unknown is where the magic happens, it's where strength is gathered. Change is the only thing in life that is constant; if you embrace it and ride the tides, you'll find that the path of least resistance is the path to true elevation.

Stacie A. Ford

Meet Stacie A. Ford, the Resilience Alchemist, a visionary business finance coach dedicated to empowering women entrepreneurs. With her unique blend of alchemy and mindset transformation, Stacie helps her clients unlock hidden financial blocks and achieve unparalleled freedom in their businesses. Her integrated approach combines ancient wisdom with modern financial strategies, guiding women to not only thrive but to transform their ventures into prosperous, liberated enterprises. Stacie takes her clients on a journey of financial alchemy to discover the true potential of their business.

Stacie is dedicated to globally helping women entrepreneurs transform their personal and business finances. With a background as a personal finance specialist, Stacie brings a wealth of experience and personal success to her coaching. She has personally eliminated over $30K in debt and replaced her six-figure nursing career salary through her ventures as a serial business owner in less than five years. Her exceptional skills and reputation as a certified financial educator and licensed personal finance specialist have earned her the prestigious role of CFO for a successful non-profit organization, The Fay Tree Foundation.

Stacie's mission as a business finance coach is to empower women entrepreneurs to achieve economic empowerment, secure their lega-

cies, and create lives of freedom and abundance. By providing transformative financial strategies and mindset coaching, she guides women
to confidently navigate their financial journeys, build prosperous businesses, and establish lasting wealth. Stacie uses a unique approach of
merging science and modern financial principles to unlock the potential within each woman to create a legacy of financial success and personal fulfillment.

http://stacieaford.com/

CHAPTER SUMMARIES

We hope you have enjoyed reading the stories of our contributing authors. Below are short chapter summaries and more about the authors, some of which offers some reflective questions for you to consider and work with after reading this book. The intention of the summaries is for you to pick up this book and be reminded of the stories so you can go back to some of the reflective questions and exercises to support your own healing and growth journey.

Anna Berardi

My voyage to self-love: when the sun rises, everything is illuminated

Anna's inspiring chapter is a tribute to the remarkable power we have to shape our own destiny. It's a 12-year journey of hope, resilience and empowerment as she overcomes a major autoimmune disease and navigates the challenges of self-doubt, burnout, despair, belief, recovery, love and motherhood. Anna was at the top of her career game, fulfilled in her work on promoting HIV/Aids prevention and human rights with UNICEF when she received a life-changing diagnosis. Her dedication and passion for work indeed masked an internal burnout. When in 2012, the universe threw her a massive curveball in the form of a scary diagnosis from her doctor, time froze, and Anna's entire world changed. For her Buddhist belief in the innate healing potential of the human body, she never let the disease define her and embraced this setback as the golden opportunity to transform her life.

Rejecting the grim prognosis of Western medicine, she embarked on an Ayurvedic intensive treatment in India that revolutionized her life. Defying conventional medicine, she turned to mind-body centred Ayurvedic practices and Buddhist faith to beat the odds. Then a flame of resilience rose in her, a phoenix rising, a lotus flower blossoming. Anna knew a deep truth: she could heal herself "her" way. Her journey took her on a quest for inner and outer healing - a holistic alchemy that resonated through the harmonious fusion of mind, body, and spirit. And along the way she found peace and joys that she had only ever imagined.

She reshaped the narrative of her diagnosis as the catalyst for a greater life expansion. Unbound by convention, her story is a testament to the indomitable fortitude of the human spirit and body to heal and forge a path forward.

Anna is a dynamic and creative change-maker whose path has always been guided by her commitment to uplifting and serving the world with her gifts. A passionate communications specialist, holistic health mentor, human rights and social justice advocate, educator mom and author with over 20 years of professional experience working to make the world a better place. She holds two master's degrees - in international education and communications - and three yoga teaching certificates. With UNAIDS and UNICEF, she has defended the human rights of kids and youth across the globe. As an educator, she has crafted innovative social studies programmes for middle and high school students. From overcoming a major autoimmune disease to becoming a visionary entrepreneur and holistic health coach, Anna is a zesty warrior at heart and a cycle breaker, embodying the spirit of positive, purpose-driven transformation.

Her path to wellness, rooted in her lifelong Buddhist belief, helped her develop a philosophy of holistic health in which body, mind, and spirit are working in harmony and thriving. Knowing that our life stories are our greatest assets, Anna's current mission is to share her healing journey and be a catalyst for change in the wider community. Now, she is on a mission to mentor others, especially young women and mothers, to ignite the limitless human potential of holistic healing, embrace the beauty of being organically imperfect and reframe the narrative of their stories.

With the motto 'We are medicine', Anna intuitively guides women to find their voice, embrace their mind-body awareness and manifest optimal holistic health. Thanks to her transformative mindset and lifestyle coaching strategies, women get to realize that a diagnosis is not a life sentence but can become the catalyst for a greater life expansion.

Inspired by her 2-year-old daughter, Anna embraces conscious parenting and aspires to found her own holistic education center fostering mindful, joyful living from the inside out. Being a lifelong Buddhist, she has acted as the leader of the SGI Buddhist Young Women's Division in her district. Proud of her southern Italian roots and in love with a healthy Mediterranean lifestyle, she is based in Spain. When she is not working, you will find her immersed in her spiritual practice, teaching yoga to kids, traveling, soaking up the sun and nature, and cherishing moments with her family.

Self-reflection exercise for the reader:

1. Is healing a destination or an ongoing journey? Reflecting on moments of healing in your life, what practices have contributed most to your emotional or spiritual growth? What shifts in mindset can help you turn dark moments into growth opportunities? Are there any specific changes you feel inspired to make in your life, particularly in embracing adversity as a pathway to personal evolution?
2. My healing journey is about embracing the beauty of being organically imperfect. How does my story inspire you to transform your inner critic into your inner guide? What imperfections in your life trouble you? How do self-doubt and perfectionism manifest in your life? How does my story inspire you to transform these feelings, what steps did I take to do so, and how can you envision that path in your own life?
3. A diagnosis can be life-changing, but my story shows that this change can be positive. Think about a time when you faced a health challenge or setback. How did it impact your outlook on life? How can you cultivate health as a practice? What opportunities can you find in it? How can it transform your life for the better?
4. Reflecting on my story, what aspects resonated most with you in terms of finding hope and inspiration amidst darkness? For example, part of my healing journey included reconnecting with my roots

in Southern Italy. We're all from different colorful places - what pieces of your identity, culture, family, or past make you feel strong, capable, and loved?

5. One of the big changes I made was balancing the yin (soft, feminine) and yang (dynamic, masculine) energies in her life. Does yin or yang energy dominate your life? How can you envision balancing the two and creating harmony?

Diane Gilman

From Princess to Pauper

Diane Gilman is a force to be reckoned with, reshaping the narrative of aging and challenging societal norms every step of the way. From her early days as a fashion rule-breaker to revolutionizing the industry with DG2 Jeans, she's proven that age is no barrier to success. At 78, Diane is just getting started on her third act, empowering women to embrace aging with confidence and vitality.

Her book, *Too Young To Be Old*, shares the electrifying story of her life and the empowering lessons she's learned along the way. From overcoming personal heartbreak to triumphing over breast cancer, Diane's journey is a testament to resilience and self-discovery. Through her podcast, *Too Young To Be Old with Diane Gilman*, she continues to inspire and educate the 50+ community on nutrition, health & wellness, beauty & skincare, and aging solutions.

With her trademark lustrous white hair and fearless sense of style, Diane is a beacon of empowerment, urging women to define their own path and embrace their true selves. Join Diane in her mission to show the world how cool aging can be and discover the limitless possibilities that come with living your best life after 50.

1. How has my writing improved your outlook on life?
2. Has my writing helped define your life goals?
3. Has my writing given you confidence to face life's challenges?
4. Has my writing given you more of a feeling of connection to a female community?
5. Has my story given you a sense of empowerment?

6. Has my story convinced you that aging can be great and the happiest years of your life?
7. What solution points in my story do you believe are most actionable in your own life?

Gabs Hayes

Gabs and her family were excitedly awaiting a new addition when she suffered the most painful loss a mother can have. Gab's healing journey was long and painful but was aided by finding the right support to help her emerge from the darkness of deep, consuming grief, and show up in the present again. Enjoy life again.

This chapter is a raw and emotional rollercoaster, taking readers on a journey of fear, loss, and ultimately, self-discovery. It opens with a stark reminder of life's fragility and the importance of living fully in the present. A near-tragic event forces Gabs to confront her deepest fears and limiting beliefs. Facing financial anxieties and emotional turmoil, she embraces vulnerability and letting go of control. Through tears and transformation, she finds a renewed sense of purpose, a thriving family dynamic, and a career that lights her soul on fire, proving that even in the darkest moments, there's the potential to create a life overflowing with joy and meaning.

But healing is not a straight road, and other challenges lay waiting in the wings, including the health of Gab's youngest child. As Gabs overcame each hurdle life put in her way, she healed more than her heart. Along the way, she confronted some painful truths about herself and discovered the power of Human Design. By getting to know herself better, show herself more compassion, Gab fully stepped into herself.

Now, Gabs empowers women through engaging podcast episodes, personalized 1:1 strategy sessions and dynamic workshop facilitation. She equips women with powerful strategies to tackle the "not enough" feeling, replace self-doubt with unwavering confidence, and craft a life full of intention and fulfillment. Beyond her career endeavors,

Gabs was once a corporate climber held back from her dreams by fear of failure and the need to please others. Despite success and a beautiful family, she felt invisible, constantly on the go yet never truly present. Overwhelm and self-doubt kept her stuck. Through deep exploration of mindset and healthy boundaries, Gabs silenced her inner critic, conquered her fears, and stepped into her power.

Gabs Hayes is a Mindset & Lifestyle Strategist, author, and speaker. She's the founder of the Balance is Bullsh!t movement, empowering women globally to ditch the overwhelm of life's messy seasons and create space for what truly matters. She's also the co-founder of The Brave Start, an all-in-one system for Product Development professionals to launch thriving coaching and consulting businesses.

Gabs cherishes time spent traveling with her kids, getting lost in books, and revitalizing her spirit at music festivals.

Questions for Inner Work:

1. What thought or situation instantly makes you feel "not enough"? How can you carry more self-compassion in those moments?
2. Where in your life do you feel most disconnected? How can you bring yourself back to your present self?
3. What masks do you wear to hide your true self? What would it take to let them go?
4. What fear holds you back from being truly open and vulnerable? If fear wasn't a factor, what change would you make to your life today?

Linda Clarke

I Am Here is the story of a six-year journey of navigating loss, depression, grief, motherhood, hope and love.

Linda was blindsided when after four years of marriage and a child together her husband announced that he thought it was 'time they separated'. Linda felt that she had failed as a mum and that sense of shame was too much to bear. Driving Linda to take a fateful drive to the beach, with one thought in mind...

But there was one emotion that was stronger than her sense of despair. Linda's love for her son. Realizing she needed professional help for her deep depression, Linda sought out that help and along the way discovered a new passion and launched her own run coaching business. Then, came the dips in the rollercoaster of life, with more loss and grief on that tough ride. But like the marathon runner that she is, Linda dug deep to find the grit to keep going on her journey and bring her light to this world.

Cry, with the knowledge that another woman has gone through it and is here to tell her story. My biggest takeaway from my chapter is coming to terms with you are greater than the experiences you endure. You are not getting over it. You are getting through it. At the end of the tunnel, a beautiful version of yourself is waiting.

It is a reflection of the hardships I experienced during the most difficult time in my life and the encounters on that journey which allow me to share my story today.

Kim Blythe

My Awakening: The Unveiling of Buried Memories is Kim's story of uncovering lost memories of childhood abuse and supressed memories.

This chapter reveals what happened when repressed memories of sexual trauma were awakened one day unexpectedly. The story shares the past of mother and daughter and how their lives ran parallel in many ways, despite her mother's efforts to create a different narrative for her daughter. Raised by a mom who was desperate for her children to lead a better life than hers, Kim strived to be independent, make her mother proud and earn affection. It elaborates on the darkness remembered by Kim and how it affected her life, her family and her career. hunger for affection that was exploited by her stepdad. Early on, she learned to beat down her own needs and emotions, and set her focus firmly on pleasing others, a behavior that Kim took into adulthood and led her to make choices that set her on a path similar to her mother's life. The key to Kim's healing and rise to glittering business success was an understanding of her mother's experience and forgiveness of an awful crime committed against a vulnerable little girl.

She shares not only the difficult moments before therapy, but also the brighter days revealed after sharing her truth. Kim hopes women are empowered to diffuse the stigma attached to speaking up about a topic so personal and uncomfortable. By shattering the stigmas associated with this type of trauma, maybe more women will find their truth sooner than Kim did.

Kim's life may have started in tough circumstances, but this woman is a testimony that we do not have to continue the hardships and struggles paved by our family's past.

Today Kim is a highly accomplished businesswoman who stands out for her achievements, professional acumen, tenacity, and award-winning career. She is a true Boss lady. Kim Blythe is a highly accomplished sales visionary, empowerment expert, business trailblazer and author with over 30 years of experience in real estate and franchise sales. President of Jan Pro Franchise Development Charlotte, NC region, a passionate and authentic woman embodying a unique blend of strength and warmth. Once you meet Kim in person, you can count on a good laugh, having fun and chatting about life and her passion for supporting other women on the path of healing and transformation.

Kim's mission is two-fold–to diffuse the stigma that makes sexual trauma a taboo topic while helping women of all ages realize trauma is not a life sentence. "She believed she could, so she did" quote, adorns her office as a daily reminder of Kim's journey to empower women to shed the secrets and shame associated with trauma

She firmly believes in the power of mentorship and practices a pay-it-forward mentality. Kim's pursuit of excellence in sales, coaching, and business ownership has not gone unnoticed. A two-time winner of the "Office of the Year" and the prestigious Lifetime Achievement awards exemplifies her dedication to her career and business.

1. Do you believe your voice has the power (speaking with intent out loud) to manifest personal and professional goals?
2. Have you experienced trauma in your life and never shared your story with anyone? And can you imagine how empowered you may feel after shedding the shame?
3. What can you do to help diffuse the stigma surrounding trauma so the uncomfortable conversations can begin sooner rather than later?
4. Is it possible that the darkness in your life (abuse, loss, trauma, disease) created a stronger woman that is now more equipped to do amazing things you never imagined you could?
5. What if you could change just one woman's life by sharing your story—your truth?

Ana Santos

Ana Santos is a money mindset coach, accountant, tax expert, speaker, published author, and successful entrepreneur. Her chapter tells the reader a little bit about her story and the outside factors that made her conscious that she was different. How and Why she wanted to become invisible and the road she travelled to discover who she really was and to accept herself for whom she really was and stop comparing herself to others. Her truly inspiring story and the road to self-acceptance and the challenges she had to overcome are the main highlight. She shares her journey and the road of self-development and acceptance that helped her reevaluate self-worth and inner beauty. I love myself; I accept myself. I'm ready for the Road Ahead of Me.

Here are five questions for the reader to reflect on after reading Ana's story:

1. How do Ana's experiences with bullying and societal pressures to conform to certain beauty standards resonate with your own experiences or observations?

2. Consider Ana's journey towards self-acceptance and self-love. Have you ever struggled with accepting yourself as you are, and if so, what steps have you taken or could take to overcome these challenges?

3. Ana mentions the importance of forgiveness in her healing process, including forgiving herself and those who harmed her. How does forgiveness play a role in your own journey towards healing and self-discovery?

4. Reflect on the significance of Ana's decision to pursue a career in accounting and her dedication to academic achievement. How have your own career aspirations or educational pursuits shaped your identity and sense of self-worth?

5. Ana's story highlights the transformative power of self-reflection and personal growth. In what ways has Ana's journey inspired you to reflect on your own life experiences and embrace the process of growth and self-discovery?

Tajni Diller

Echoes of Loss: Beyond Shadows and into Light, reveals her journey through personal loss and survivor's guilt, showcasing her strength and commitment to healing. Her story is not just one of personal success but a testament to the power of faith, resilience and the impact of supportive relationships in navigating life's toughest challenges. She aims to inspire others, especially women, to recognize their worth, embrace their potential, and achieve their dreams, underpinned by a belief in the transformative power of open financial discussions and education. Tajni's life story is one of determination and dedication.

From becoming a wife and mother at 17 to establishing herself as a solopreneur by 25, she has navigated numerous roles with grace and determination. In her gripping story Tajni shares the most personal story of loss of her daughter, how it has impacted her and her family's lives. She candidly shares her innermost personal journey of overcoming loss, grief and depressions. Her life had twists and turns but in her mid-40's she completed her college education and around that same time became a business owner and a pastor. Today, she is not only a Certified Tax Coach and Fractional CFO, but also the visionary founder of Boutique Books LLC, a revolutionary bookkeeping firm designed to empower small and medium-sized businesses. Her leadership extends into her community where she serves as a credentialed pastor and an international speaker, sharing her insights and inspiring others to overcome their financial challenges.

Stephanie Myers

Stephanie Myers is a seasoned advocate and change-maker with over two decades of experience in male-dominated industries. Raised in an environment that often relegated women to second-class status, Stephanie was inspired by her mother, Mary, a resolute and competent woman who taught her to value her own strengths and individuality beyond societal expectations. This foundational belief fueled Stephanie's determination to alter the narrative for herself and other women striving to make their mark.

As an advocate for gender equity globally, Stephanie believes that exposing and challenging the biases women face is essential to the fight for gender equality. Her work serves as both a testimony and a guide, helping others recognize that women are capable of achieving anything they set their minds to and should be afforded the same privileges—recognition, compensation, and opportunities—that their male counterparts often receive.

My name is Stephanie Myers aka Bias Breaking Beauty. I stress the need for women to use their voice to challenge the biases faced in the workplace, in business, and in society at large. I want all of us to be empowered to be ourselves and walk in our own truth. No apologies needed and none given for being the women that you are! Collectively, we are unstoppable, and it is time the world recognizes women and our priceless value as an equal member of society. Join me and together we move gender equity forward never looking back!

Emily Sanders

The Sixteen-Year-Old Girl Inside Me...

In her chapter, Emily pays homage to her sixteen-year-old self by outlining the events of a single evening that forever altered her life goals and dreams following a traumatic rape. These events empowered her to chase her aspirations, ultimately leading her to compete for and win the title of Miss Colorado for America 2021. The healing she derived from writing this chapter has fueled her ambition to engage with Colorado lawmakers. She aims to advocate for a more comprehensive sex education curriculum, including safe dating practices and confidence in relationships, driven by a desire to foster greater awareness and understanding.

As a teenager, I viewed my little section of the world through rose-colored glasses, making everything seem safe and happy-go-lucky. Believing nothing was impossible, I had big plans to chase even bigger dreams. However, the unknown ugliness in the world lurked around the corner, detouring me from every plan I had.

Emily is the Queen of the Bounce-Back, continually reinventing herself. She embodies the spirit of resilience and ambition, a testament to the transformative power of following one's passions and dreams. Fueled by her desire to someday work as a professional dancer, she immersed herself in the world of competitive dance, and later she found herself at the age of 21, becoming an iconic Vegas Showgirl. Now, she is a mother of two wonderful children, embracing roles as a dance mom and a lacrosse mom, and finds fulfillment working in business development and coaching entrepreneurial minded practitioners in the wellness sector.

With a newfound passion for writing, she plans to continue expanding her portfolio, contributing to both books and magazines, as she embraces this exciting new chapter in her journey. She's forever grateful for this experience and knows that this is just the tip of the iceberg.

1. Which parts of this chapter did you find most engaging or interesting, and why?
2. Were there any sections or concepts that you found difficult to read and understand? If so, please specify.
3. How did the content and the details of the attack of the chapter make you feel overall? Were there any particular sections that evoked a strong emotional response from you?
4. Did you find the information to be detailed in a way wherein you could visualize the events as you were reading them?
5. Do you feel that the content could be shared with students in a middle and high school level wherein they can identify as to the dangers associated with parties? What specific elements influenced your rating the most?

Shameria Ann Davis

Many Traumas, Unbelievable Triumph...

Would you be able to discover a jagged path to self-belief with a past like this one? In an awe-inspiring chapter, Shameria made strides in baring her soul as she talks about how she navigated through the harrowing waters of military trauma, domestic violence, and healing. In the midst of what others may call darkness, she discovers a wellspring of inner strength, resilience, and unwavering courage that propelled her forward on a path of healing and transformation. The path wasn't easy, but it was necessary.

When trauma happens, it's not the elegant writing of this chapter that unfolds; it's a messy, unassuming, unknowing and imperfectly human experience happening moment by moment. There is no recollection sometimes that the journey is in fact a series of repetitive trauma with a similar theme or otherwise. No one can see the future before it happens, right? So, one must also contend with the idea that every time adversity comes, fight or flight kicks in. If you're young, a bootstrap reaction is par for the course. The journey taught her to see the experiences for what they were, to unconsciously recover from each hardship rebelliously with a positive goal and to give her heart a soliloquy to guide her to healing.

With each obstacle she faced, Shameria emerged stronger and more determined to not only survive but to thrive in all aspects of her life. One resounding theme she aspires to convey is her faith in God, knowing without a shadow of doubt that every experience could have been worse. Prayer and a belief in a better tomorrow accompanied every experience. She was extended supernatural grace and mercy along the way and consequently, her journey is presented here to be a beacon of hope for anyone facing adversity. Her story is a present reminder that even in the darkest of times, there is light and a way forward towards a brighter tomorrow.

This chapter should provide any reader with tangible takeaways to propel themselves into healing. She lists out tips to use and questions you may desire to ask yourself if you're reeling from trauma you are not responsible for, yet must face and recover from. Blessed, resilient, courageous, and an indomitable spirit *is* Shameria Ann, today and always. Who are you?

Shameria's Questions for the readers to reflect on:

1. After listening to my account of hyper vigilance and fear, are you able to identify similar signals within yourself?

2. Have I provided you with at least some necessary resources to support your healing process?

3. Can you identify a personal experience this chapter brought to mind that might benefit from further reflection to promote healing?

4. Have you ever experienced a memory that was hidden in your subconscious, only to resurface in a peculiar manner?

5. Do you possess an impactful and significant personal narrative that, with nurturing, could potentially touch another individual? Would you consider sharing it at this moment?

Stacie A. Ford

Stacie's story is about having the courage to face health crisis, adversity, and change. It is a story of starting over, leaving comfort and embracing growth. This story is about embracing vulnerability, uncertainty, fear of failure and the importance of mental and emotional health, as it motivates women to take control of their lives, while embracing new possibilities courage and confidence

For nearly two decades Stacie A. Ford worked in healthcare as a registered nurse, a career she loved with pride and sense of accomplishment. However, before entering into her second decade as a nurse, an unforeseen circumstance, a health crisis not only ended her career, it caused anxiety, depression and near financial ruin.

Forced retirement before the age of forty wasn't a part of the plans. Stacie had to make some tough decisions on how to rebuild her life as her world had been changed mentally, physically, emotionally and financially. Years of endless medical procedures that offered no real improvements to the debilitating pain she endured, leaving her chronically depressed, she contemplated taking things into her own hands with thoughts of suicide.

The guilt of leaving her family in an emotional and financial mess made her rethink her plans. She resorted to figuring out a plan B that would not only provide a much-needed diversion from the constant worries about her future. Stacie made a decision to reinvent herself by taking courses in personal finance from home. She spent extensive time earning degrees towards various areas in personal finance and financial literacy. As a result, she ultimately learned how to get good with money. The newfound skills and resources established her confidence in a topic that many others were struggling in, money management.

During the pandemic, while the world shut down, Stacie managed to pull herself from a deep depression with a newfound passion and purpose. Her newfound knowledge helped her to pay off her home 15 years earlier than planned, eliminated over 45k in personal debt and started a financial planning side hustle. That side hustle soon turned into the fully thriving and profitable Business Finance Coaching firm Divine Wealth Solutions which focuses on coaching and educating women entrepreneurs to have the confidence and skills to obtain their money goals both personally and in business, as women are the fastest growing yet most marginalized sector of business owners. Stacie is very passionate about empowering women economically. Her motto is " A woman who is empowered with her money not only has choices she will change the world!" She is here for that change, as a woman and a business owner and author her desire to make a generational impact is her driving force!

Personal Reflection Questions

1. In what ways have your experiences with hardship and adversity led to personal growth or a transformation in your identity?
2. How do you perceive your current self compared to who you were before facing these challenges?
3. What are the most valuable lessons you have learned from overcoming hardships and reinventing yourself?
4. 4.How do you plan to apply these lessons to future challenges or to help others facing similar situations?

ABOUT WOMEN THRIVE MEDIA

Women Thrive Media -Women Thrive is a global media platform where every woman has a voice. Where every woman's story is celebrated. We recognise the impact and contribution that women make in the world, and our mission is to build a platform where every woman feels included, celebrated and proud to be part of a community like this.

We started our mission work in 2017 and have since grown to an international platform of over 600k women worldwide. Over the years, we have hosted many amazing and life-changing events, had 100s of inspiring international speakers take our stage, and thousands of attendees' lives changed or impacted by our work.

Now we pride ourselves on being an inclusive platform where women looking for guidance, support and mentorship, can come and connect with others who have already walked the walk and able to share their knowledge and wisdom. Be it through our podcast, events, book, or monthly Women Thrive magazine.

Our mission is to reach 1 MILLION women every year and create a global impact on women's empowerment because we believe that if one woman is given the confidence, tools, and resources to rise, she will go on to empower thousands more. We have seen time and time again when we, as women, come together, the impact and ripple effect is so much more powerful than a woman trying to make an impact on her own.

We hope you join our community, mission, and future events.

www.womenthrivesummit.com
www.womenthrivemagazine.com

PAY IT FORWARD

If you enjoyed this book, please consider passing it to another woman that needs to hear these stories...

Tell them:
    What was your favourite story?
    What are your biggest take aways?
    Who do you want to pass this book onto and why?

Tell them:
    What was your favourite story?
    What are your biggest take aways?
    Who do you want to pass this book onto and why?

Tell them:
    What was your favourite story?
    What are your biggest take aways?
    Who do you want to pass this book onto and why?

Made in the USA
Middletown, DE
17 December 2024

67429494R00126